PACIFIC
OVERTURES

Haruki Fujimoto in the Broadway production.

PACIFIC OVERTURES

Music and Lyrics by
STEPHEN SONDHEIM

Book by
JOHN WEIDMAN

Additional Material by Hugh Wheeler

Originally Produced and Directed
on Broadway by Harold Prince

Theatre Communications Group
1991

Pacific Overtures is published by Theatre Communications Group, Inc.,
355 Lexington Ave., New York, NY 10017.

TCG gratefully acknowledges public funds from the National Endowment for the
Arts and the New York State Council on the Arts in addition to the generous support
of the following foundations and corporations: Alcoa Foundation; Ameritech Foun-
dation; ARCO Foundation; AT&T Foundation; Citibank; ConAgra Charitable Foun-
dation; Consolidated Edison Company of New York; Nathan Cummings Foundation;
Dayton Hudson Foundation; Exxon Corporation; Ford Foundation; James Irvine
Foundation; Jerome Foundation; Andrew W. Mellon Foundation; Metropolitan Life
Foundation; National Broadcasting Company; Pew Charitable Trusts; Philip Morris
Companies; Scherman Foundation; Shell Oil Company Foundation; Shubert
Foundation.

Cover: Ernest Abuba in the 1984 Off Broadway revival of *Pacific Overtures*.
All photographs by Martha Swope.

Sondheim, Stephen.
[Pacific overtures. Libretto]
Pacific overtures / music and lyrics by Stephen Sondheim ; book by
John Weidman ; additional material by Hugh Wheeler.
ISBN 1-55936-025-9 (cloth). — ISBN 1-55936-026-7 (pbk.)
1. Musical—Librettos.   I. Weidman, John, 1946-
II. Wheeler, Hugh, 1912-   III. Title.
ML50.S705P3 1991 [Case]
782.1'4'0268—dc20   90-29041
CIP
MN
Design and composition by The Sarabande Press
First TCG Edition, June 1991

Pacific Overtures was first presented by Harold Prince in association with Ruth Mitchell at the Winter Garden Theatre, New York City, on January 11, 1976. Scenery by Boris Aronson, costumes by Florence Klotz, lighting by Tharon Musser, orchestrations by Jonathan Tunick, choreography by Patricia Birch and direction by Harold Prince. The cast was as follows:

RECITER/SHOGUN/ JONATHAN GOBLE	*Mako*
ABE, FIRST COUNCILLOR	*Yuki Shimoda*
MANJIRO	*Sab Shimono*
SECOND COUNCILLOR/OLD MAN/FRENCH ADMIRAL	*James Dybas*
SHOGUN'S MOTHER/ MERCHANT/AMERICAN ADMIRAL	*Alvin Ing*
THIRD COUNCILLOR/ SAMURAI'S DAUGHTER	*Freddy Mao*
KAYAMA	*Isao Sato*
TAMATE (KAYAMA'S WIFE)/ SAMURAI/STORYTELLER/ SWORDSMAN	*Soon-Teck Oh*
SERVANT/COMMODORE MATTHEW CALBRAITH PERRY	*Haruki Fujimoto*
OBSERVERS	*Alvin Ing, Ricardo Tobia*
FISHERMAN/WRESTLER/LORD OF THE SOUTH	*Jae Woo Lee*
SON/PRIEST/NOBLE	*Timm Fujii*
GRANDMOTHER/WRESTLER/ JAPANESE MERCHANT	*Conrad Yama*
THIEF/SAMURAI/ SOOTHSAYER/WARRIOR/ RUSSIAN ADMIRAL	*Mark Hsu Syers*

ADAMS/SAMURAI/NOBLE	Ernest Abuba
WILLIAMS/LORD OF THE SOUTH	Larry Hama
SHOGUN'S WIFE	Freda Foh Shen
PHYSICIAN/MADAM/BRITISH ADMIRAL	Ernest Harada
PRIEST/BOY	Gedde Watanabe
SHOGUN'S COMPANION/ DUTCH ADMIRAL	Patrick Kinser-Lau
GIRLS	Timm Fujii, Patrick Kinser-Lau, Gedde Watanabe, Leslie Watanabe
IMPERIAL PRIEST	Tom Matsusaka
BRITISH SAILORS	Timm Fujii, Patrick Kinser-Lau, Mark Hsu Syers
MUSICIANS	Fusako Yoshida, Genji Ito

SERVANTS, SAILORS, TOWNSPEOPLE: *Susan Kikuchi, Diane Lam, Kim Miyori, Freda Foh Shen, Kenneth S. Eiland, Timm Fujii, Joey Ginza, Patrick Kinser-Lau, Tony Marinyo, Kevin Maung, Dingo Secretario, Mark Hsu Syers, Ricardo Tobia, Gedde Watanabe, Leslie Watanabe*

The revised version of *Pacific Overtures* was first presented by The Shubert Organization and McCann & Nugent at the Promenade Theatre, New York City, on October 12, 1984. Scenery by James Morgan, costumes by Mark Passerell, additional costumes by Eiko Yamaguchi, lighting by Mary Jo Dondlinger, orchestrations by James Stenborg, choreography by Janet Watson and direction by Fran Soeder. The cast was as follows:

RECITER	*Ernest Abuba*
ABE	*Tony Marino*
SHOGUN'S MOTHER/BRITISH ADMIRAL	*Chuck Brown*
KAYAMA	*Kevin Gray*
TAMATE/BRITISH SAILOR	*Timm Fujii*
MANJIRO/FISHERMAN/ FRENCH ADMIRAL	*John Caleb*
MERCHANT	*Ronald Yamamoto*
THIEF	*Tim Ewing*
COMMODORE MATTHEW CALBRAITH PERRY	*John Bantay*
MADAM/RUSSIAN ADMIRAL	*Thomas Ikeda*
OLD MAN/AMERICAN ADMIRAL	*John Baray*
BOY/DUTCH ADMIRAL/ BRITISH SAILOR	*Francis Jue*
WARRIOR/BRITISH SAILOR	*Ray Contreras*
IMPERIAL PRIEST	*Tom Matsusaka*
SAMURAI'S DAUGHTER	*Allan Tung*
SERVANTS	*Gerri Igarashi, Gayln Kong, Diane Lam, Christine Toy*

Ernest Harada and Timm Fujii in the Broadway production.

NOTE

Pacific Overtures borrows liberally from the techniques of the Japanese *kabuki* theater in every aspect of its production and performance. Freely adapted for use on the American musical stage, these techniques include the playing of women's roles by men; the use of a *Reciter,* who alternately comments on the action, joins it, or speaks in place of one of the other characters; the presence of a *hanamichi,* or runway, which allows performers to make entrances and exits through the house; and the changing of props and costumes onstage by a group of stagehands clad in black. Black being the color of non-existence, these stagehands are literally invisible as far as a Japanese audience is concerned.

ACT I

Yuki Shimoda and Freddy Mao in the Broadway production.

SCENE 1

Three Japanese Musicians enter and take positions on a low platform at the side of the stage. One plays briefly on the shamisen and sings. From Offstage comes the sound of a bass drum beaten furiously and then wooden blocks sharply striking the floor.

The stage and the auditorium go to black.

The stage and house lights bump up revealing the Reciter in front of the show curtain, forehead touching the floor in prayer. The blocks are struck again.

RECITER: Nippon. The Floating Kingdom. An island empire which for centuries has lived in perfect peace, undisturbed by intruders from across the sea. There was a time when foreigners were welcome here, but they took advantage of our friendship. Two hundred and fifty years ago we drove them out—by sacred decree of the great Shogun Tokugawa—and ordered them never again to set foot on our ancestral soil. From then until this day, in the month of July, eighteen hundred and fifty-three, there has been nothing to threaten the serene and changeless cycle of our days.

(A Stagehand runs the show curtain across the stage, revealing the Members of the Company. They are a cross-section of mid-nineteenth-century Japanese society, everything from farmers to samurai. Music from the pit orchestra. The Reciter sings)

In the middle of the world we float
In the middle of the sea.
The realities remain remote
In the middle of the sea.
Kings are burning somewhere,
Wheels are turning somewhere,
Trains are being run,
Wars are being won,
Things are being done
Somewhere out there, not here.
Here we paint screens.

(The Company demonstrates)

Yes . . . the arrangement of the screens:
We sit inside the screens
And contemplate the view
That's painted on the screens
More beautiful than true.
Beyond the screens
That glide aside
Are further screens
That open wide
With scenes of screens like the ones that glide.
And no one presses in,
And no one glances out,
And kings are burning somewhere,

ALL: Not here!

As the hurricanes have come, they've passed
In the middle of the sea.
The advantages are made to last
In the middle of the sea.
Gods are crumbling somewhere,
Machines are rumbling somewhere,
Ways are being found,

Watches being wound,
Prophets being crowned
Somewhere out there, not here.
Here we plant rice.

RECITER: Yes. The arrangement of the rice:

(The Company demonstrates)

The farmer plants the rice.
The priest exalts the rice.
The Lord collects the rice.
The merchant buys the rice.
The craftsman makes the sword
And sells it to the lord
And buys at twice the former price
What he counts on his lord to protect with his sword:

ALL: The rice!

RECITER:
    They eat the rice and then
    The day begins again,
ALL:
    And gods are crumbling somewhere—
    Not here!

The disturbances are worlds away
In the middle of the sea.
And tomorrow will be like today
In the middle of the sea.
Blood is flowing somewhere,
Ideas are growing somewhere,
Trails are being blazed,
Voices being raised,
Women being praised
Somewhere out there, not here.
Here we trade bows.

RECITER: Yes. The arrangement of the bows:

(Two Stagehands enter carrying a tiny puppet dressed in regal robes. Everyone immediately drops to the ground, forehead down)

First for the Emperor,
Descendant of the sun-goddess Amaterasu!
All-knowing and all-powerful!
Ruler absolute!
One year old.

(As the puppet/Emperor is carried off, Two Bearers enter and cross the stage carrying a curtained palanquin)

Second for the Shogun,
Protector of the kingdom,
Keeper of the peace.
Seldom seen.

(As the Bearers exit, Two Feudal Lords swagger on)

Then for the Lords of the South,
Vassals to the Shogun,
Loyal to their master . . .
Not for long.

(The Two Lords exit as everyone stands)

And kings are burning somewhere,

ALL: Not here!

The advantages go on and on
In the middle of the sea.
As the centuries have come, they've gone
In the middle of the sea.
Days arise to be replaced,
Lines are drawn and lines erased.
Life and death are but verses in a poem.

Out there blood flows.
Who knows?
Here we paint screens,

GROUP A:
Plant the rice,

GROUP B:
Arrange the flowers,

GROUP A:
View the moon,

GROUP B:
Exchange the gifts,

GROUP A:
Plant the rice,

ALL:
Arrange tomorrow like today to float,
Slide the screens,
Exchange the poems,
Stir the tea,
Exchange the bows,
Plant the rice,
Arrange tomorrow to be like today,
To float. . . *(Slowly they begin to leave the stage)*

GROUP A:	GROUP B:
The viewing of the moon,	The viewing of the moon,
The planting of the rice,	The planting of the rice,
The stirring of the tea,	The stirring of the tea,
The painting of the	The painting of the
screens.	screens.
	We float.
The viewing of the moon,	
	The stirring of the tea,

7

The planting of the rice,   The folding of the fans.
The weaving of the mats.   We float.
    The placing of the stones,
We float.   The painting of the sliding
      screens,
The viewing of the moon,   The wrapping of the gifts,
The planting of the rice,   The sliding of the painted
      screens.
The catching of the fish,   We float.
    The weaving of the mats,
The painting of . . .   The stirring of the tea,
We float . . .   We float . . .

(The Last Member of the Company exits, leaving the Reciter alone on stage)

RECITER: We float.

(Speaks)

Even in a land of changeless order, there are sometimes slight—disturbances. Nothing of importance, nothing threatening or distressing. A piece of gossip from a noodle seller, or the languorous whisper of a geisha. "I hear . . . I heard . . . The rice merchant is sure . . ." Just a rumor, to be noted—and dismissed. Nothing of importance, nothing—but wait, there is another rumor! "Who? . . . And where? . . . You say you saw the cage yourself?"

(A procession down the hanamichi: Two Bearers carrying a cage/palanquin, in which a Japanese in Western sailor's dress sits crouched. The Sailor may be played by an actor or represented by an articulated dummy)

A prisoner in Western dress, conveyed to Edo in the dead of night. There to be examined by the mighty

Shogun himself, surrogate to an emperor far too holy to be sullied by mortal eyes. The Shogun!

(A curtain drops, revealing the Shogun's court. Present are Lord Abe, First Councilor to the Shogun, the Second and Third Councilors to the Shogun, and the Shogun's Mother. The Shogun is absent)

Oh dear, no Shogun. Perhaps his stars today are inauspicious for an audience.

(The Bearers carry the cage/palanquin into the court and put it down)

ABE: The prisoner's name?

THIRD COUNCILOR: Manjiro, my lord.

ABE: Where does he come from?

RECITER: The questioner is Lord Abe, first councilor to the absent Shogun.

THIRD COUNCILOR: Nakahama, lord. A fishing village on the south coast of Shikoku.

ABE: And do all the residents of Nakahama wear such foreign dress?

THIRD COUNCILOR: No, my lord.

ABE: Then you will explain his appearance.

THIRD COUNCILOR *(Reading from a scroll)*: He is a fisherman, my lord. Six years ago his boat was driven out to sea by storms. He was rescued by the captain of a barbarian ship, who took him to a place called Massachusetts, where he went to school. From there—

MOTHER *(Interrupting)*: What does this mean?

RECITER: The Shogun's mother.

THIRD COUNCILOR: That he has come here from America.

MOTHER: America?

SECOND COUNCILOR: But why has he come back? Does he not know that he has violated our laws twice—first when he left Japan, and then when he returned? Each crime is punishable by death.

(To Manjiro)

Why have you come back?

RECITER *(Speaking for Manjiro)*: There were rumors in America, my lord. Rumors which I thought my countrymen should hear.

SECOND COUNCILOR: What did the rumors say?

RECITER *(For Manjiro)*: That America would send an expedition to Japan.

ABE *(Carefully)*: And are these rumors true?

RECITER *(For Manjiro)*: They are, my lord. As I made my way back home I stopped at Okinawa. In the harbor there were four black ships, Western warships, fitted out with giant cannon, manned by sailors, armed with weapons such as you have never seen. Americans, my lord, and their ships are coming here!

THIRD COUNCILOR: It is obvious. The man is a traitor, sent here by the Westerners to spy on us.

RECITER *(For Manjiro)*: My lord, I'm not! I swear to you! Even as we speak the ships are on their way. You must prepare yourselves to deal with them. You must—

THIRD COUNCILOR *(Interrupting)*: You dare to tell Lord Abe what to do!

RECITER *(For Manjiro)*: My lord, I—

THIRD COUNCILOR: You dare suggest that we meet face to face with Western dogs!

SECOND COUNCILOR: That we subject ourselves to such humiliation!

ABE: If he saw the ships at Okinawa, they will be here—any day.

(Abe gestures and the Bearers exit with Manjiro's cage)

When the Americans arrive, someone will have to deal with them. Someone, but who?

(On another playing area, a young Samurai enters, followed by his Wife)

RECITER: Kayama Yesaemon. A samurai, but one of little consequence. He and his wife Tamate have been fishing. This year they cast their nets in streams belonging to the Shogun. A transgression to be sure, but one well worth the risk, for they have caught the lucky ayu, a fish which portends one year of good fortune.

(Two Samurai appear and block Kayama's path)

FIRST SAMURAI: Kayama Yesaemon?

(Kayama nods)

SECOND SAMURAI: You are wanted by the Shogun's Councilors.

FIRST SAMURAI: You are to come with us at once.

KAYAMA: But why? I—

SECOND SAMURAI *(Interrupting)*: It is not your business to ask why.

(Kayama bows and turns to Tamate)

KAYAMA: Wait for me, Tamate. Wait at home.

TAMATE *(Urgently)*: Tell them that we meant no harm. Tell them—

KAYAMA *(Interrupting)*: Wait for me at home.

(Tamate exits as Kayama turns and steps from his playing area into the Shogun's court. He prostrates himself before Lord Abe)

ABE: Kayama Yesaemon?

KAYAMA: Yes, my lord.

ABE: Your rank?

KAYAMA: Secretary to the Governor of Uraga. And if in some way I have offended—

SECOND COUNCILOR: Silence!

THIRD COUNCILOR: Hold your tongue!

KAYAMA *(Humiliated)*: Yes, my lord.

ABE: From today you have become Prefect of Police for the entire city of Uraga.

KAYAMA: I—I have? My lord, I humbly thank you for this great honor and will do all in my power to be worthy of your trust!

ABE: Yes—you will!

RECITER: A haiku:

> A gift unearned
> And unexpected
> Often has a hidden price.

ABE: And so, when the Americans arrive, you will take a boat to their ships and you will order them to return immediately from whence they came. Is that understood?

KAYAMA: I ... my lord ... in a boat, my lord ... ordering. . . ?

ABE: You will inform them of the sacred decree. You will terrify them with the fate that awaits all foreign devils who dare to set foot on our holy soil. Kayama Yesaemon, may the Gods of our fathers make you equal to this awesome task!

SCENE 2

A small Japanese house is revealed Upstage. The Court exits. Kayama walks into the house, where he is joined by Tamate.

TAMATE: What did the Councilors say?

KAYAMA: They have appointed me Prefect of Police of the city of Uraga.

TAMATE: But, this is wonderful, to receive such happy news when we expected—

KAYAMA *(Interrupting)*: It is not happy news, Tamate. There are foreign warships on their way to Japan. They will first be sighted off Uraga, and it will be the duty of the Prefect of Police to go out to meet them— and drive them away.

TAMATE: But how—if they are so powerful?

KAYAMA: I do not know.

TAMATE: And if they refuse to go. . . ?

KAYAMA: It will be great disgrace, so great that no one near the Shogun's throne would dare to deal with these barbarians. That is the only reason why I have been chosen.

TAMATE *(Pause)*: Perhaps the foreigners will not come.

KAYAMA: They will come. And should I fail, you know what we must do.

(Kayama begins to remove his short sword from its sheath and Tamate starts up in alarm. Suddenly a bell sounds in the distance)

The Americans are here!

(A shakuhachi plays a mournful solo. Two Observers appear. Tamate dances as the Observers sing. The First sings about her, the Second sings her words and thoughts)

FIRST OBSERVER:
The eye sees, the thought flies.
The eye tells, the thought denies.

SECOND OBSERVER:
I will prepare for your returning.
(Is there no other way?)

13

FIRST OBSERVER:
> The word falls, the heart cries.
> The heart knows the word's disguise.

SECOND OBSERVER:
> I shall expect you then at evening.
> (Is there no other way?)

FIRST OBSERVER:
> The bird sings, the wind sighs,
> The air stirs, the bird shies.
> A storm approaches.

SECOND OBSERVER:
> (There must be other ways . . .)

FIRST OBSERVER:
> The leaf shakes, the wings rise.
> The song stops, the bird flies.
> The storm approaches.

SECOND OBSERVER:
> I will have supper waiting.

FIRST OBSERVER:
> The song stops, the bird flies.
> The mind stirs, the heart replies,
> "There is no other way."
> "There is no other way."

SECOND OBSERVER:
> I will prepare for your return.
> I shall expect you then at evening.

(The bells sound again. Tamate pauses before Kayama. He hesitates, then turns quickly on his heel and exits)

FIRST OBSERVER:
> The word stops, the heart dies.

The wind counts the lost goodbyes.

SECOND OBSERVER:
>There is no other way.
>There is no other way.

>*(Tamate takes a sheathed knife from the household shrine, kneels, pulls the knife halfway out, then looks up sharply as the bells sound once more)*

SCENE 3

An enormous bell is lowered from the flies, and a Fisherman rushes on and pumps it wildly.

FISHERMAN *(Sings)*:
>I was standing on the beach
>Near the cliffs
>At Oshima.
>I was spreading out the nets
>For the morning sun.
>It was early in July
>And the day was getting hot,
>And I stopped to wipe my eyes,
>And by accident I turned
>And looked out to sea . . .
>
>And there came,
>Breaking through the mist,
>Roaring through the sea,
>Four black dragons,
>Spitting fire.
>And I ran,
>Cursing through the fields,
>Calling the alarm,

Shouting to the world,
"Four black dragons!
Spitting fire!"
And the earth trembled,
And the sky cracked,
And I thought it was the end of the world.

(A Merchant and his Family enter. The Fisherman returns to the bell. The Merchant leads a horse, which is loaded down with sacks and boxes)

MERCHANT: Come! Come quickly! Hurry up! Come!

(He looks out front, sees the approach of the Western warships)

Ah! Come on!

(The Merchant's Son also carries a number of bundles, and in his haste he trips and drops them)

MERCHANT: Pick them up, you clumsy oaf! No, wait! Come take these instead!

(He hands his Son several lacquer boxes)

And hurry! If we are not out of here before the barbarians come, they will kill us all!

SON *(Trying to tie the boxes on the horse)*: The horse is loaded, father. There is room for nothing else.

MERCHANT: What? Leave my fortune here to be destroyed by foreign dogs! I'll stay and fight before—

(He is interrupted by underscoring, indicating the approaching invaders)

Quick! Grab the horse's reins! No, get your grandmother! There is no time to lose! All right then. Everybody ready?

(The Grandmother doesn't move)

GRANDMOTHER: A mother does not walk. She rides.

MERCHANT: What!

GRANDMOTHER: A mother does not walk. She rides.

MERCHANT: But the horse's legs are buckling as it is!

GRANDMOTHER: A mother does not—

MERCHANT *(Interrupting)*: All right, all right!

(Gesturing to his son)

Here, push those sacks aside.

(They try to hoist the Grandmother up on the horse, but it trembles under the weight, then drops down to its knees)

You see? You will have to walk with the rest of us.

GRANDMOTHER: I would rather stay behind and be ravished by the barbarians.

MERCHANT *(Exasperated)*: As you wish. Come on then! Come!

(The family turns to go)

RECITER: Confucius tells the story of a merchant who grew tired of caring for his aged mother. He called his son and told him to prepare a litter, so that they might carry the feeble old woman out to the countryside to die. The young boy set to work, and when the man returned, he found his son had built, not one litter, but two. "The first one is for grandmother," explained the boy, "and the second I shall save and use when you have grown as old as she is."

MERCHANT: Oh, all right! Come on then!

(He throws his Mother on his back and the Entire Family rushes off pell mell)

Come!

(A Thief enters as they leave)

THIEF *(Sings)*:
> I was rifling through the house
> Of some priests
> In Uraga.
> It was only after dawn,
> They were sleeping still.
> I had finished with the silks,
> I was hunting for the gold,
> When I heard them getting up,
> So I bolted through a door . . .
> Which looked out to sea . . .

FISHERMAN:
> And there came . . .

THIEF:
> And there came . . .

FISHERMAN:
> Breaking through the mist . . .

THIEF:
> Boiling through the mist . . .

FISHERMAN:
> Roaring through the sea . . .

THIEF:
> Rising from the sea . . .

FISHERMAN:
> Four black dragons . . .

THIEF:
> Four volcanoes . . .

FISHERMAN:
> Spitting fire . . .

THIEF:
> Spitting fire!
> And I ran . . .

FISHERMAN:
> And I ran . . .

THIEF:
> Cursing down the halls . . .

FISHERMAN:
> Cursing through the fields . . .

THIEF:
> Shouting to the priests . . .

FISHERMAN:
> Shouting to the world . . .

BOTH:
> "Notify the gods!

THIEF:	FISHERMAN:
Four volcanoes, Spitting fire!"	Four black dragons, Spitting fire!"

RECITER *(Sings, very quietly)*:
> And the feet pattered
> As the men came down to stare,
> And the women started screaming
> Like the gulls.
> Hai!
> Hai!

(Each time the Reciter gives his small scream, Townspeople appear, delicately showing alarm. They stare, point, and as the panic grows, run bewilderedly. The effect should be one of a Japanese watercolor riot)

And they crowded into temples
And they flapped about the square—
Hai!—
Like the gulls.
Hai!

TOWNSPEOPLE:
Hai! Hai!
Four black dragons,
Spitting fire!

RECITER:
Then the hooves clattered
And the warriors were there,
Diving quickly through the panic
Like the gulls.
Hai!
Hai!
And the swords were things of beauty
As they glided through the air—
Hai!
Like the gulls.
Hai!

TOWNSPEOPLE:
Hai! Hai!
Four black dragons,
Spitting fire!

THIEF	FISHERMAN
And the sun darkened	I had seen
And the sea bubbled	Dragons before,
And the earth trembled	Never so many,
And the sky cracked	Never like these,
And I thought it was the end	And I thought it was the end
Of the world!	Of the world!

THIEF *(Snatching a lacquer box from a bag carried by a fleeing Townsman)*: If I don't take it, the barbarians will. What does it matter, anyway? Whoever these invaders are, they can be no worse than the merchants who have bled us dry, or the samurai who cut us down in the street if we fail to bow when they go by.

(A Samurai enters and surprises the Thief, who drops to his knees and tries to conceal his stolen goods. The Samurai draws his sword and lops off the Thief's hand)

GROUP A:	GROUP B:
And the sun darkened	I had seen
And the sea bubbled	Dragons before,
And the earth trembled	Never so many,
And the sky cracked,	Never like these,
And I thought it was the end	And I thought it was the end
Of the world!	Of the world!

(Behind the frozen Townspeople, the U.S.S. Powhatan *appears and begins moving ominously Downstage. The Townspeople panic and run off in all directions)*

RECITER:
And it was.

SCENE 4

The deck of the U.S.S. Powhatan. *Sailors, extravagantly stylized like fairy-tale ogres, stand at attention. Behind them, equally bizarre and scary, stand Two Officers.*

RECITER: They come from a land of mystery behind the setting sun. Barbarians with hooked noses like mountain imps. Giants with wild, coarse hair and faces grey as the dead. Americans! Look how they glare!

(Suddenly all the Sailors raise their guns and aim them at the audience)

Look how they aim their sorcerer's weapons directly at us!

(A sudden spot reveals Commodore Matthew Calbraith Perry, isolated in some conspicuous position on deck. He is a lionlike figure of terror from a child's dream, complete with flowing white mane)

Oh, look! Their leader! Commodore Matthew Calbraith Perry! Surely he is the King of the Demons come to strike us blind and to devour our children!

(Perry makes a sudden, extravagantly threatening gesture)

In this darkest hour, who will save Japan?

(Kayama appears, crouching in a tiny guard boat which approaches the U.S.S. Powhatan. *He is so inconspicuous that the sailors don't even notice him)*

KAYAMA: Please. I am here.

(Still no attention)

Please!

(Suddenly one of the Officers swivels to him aiming his gun)

FIRST OFFICER *(Barking.* NOTE: *The Americans speak in a terse, stylized pidgin English)*: Boat go! No boats here.
KAYAMA: But—
FIRST OFFICER: Go!

KAYAMA: I will not go. I am the Prefect of Police of the city of Uraga and I say: You must not stay here. Our laws forbid it.

FIRST OFFICER: You hear. I say . . . no boats. Go . . . or . . .

(Shouting)

Bang!

(A Second Officer, attracted by the sound, joins him, peering down)

SECOND OFFICER: What is here?

KAYAMA: My lord, I have orders. You must go away. There is a sacred decree. No foreigner can come to our land.

SECOND OFFICER: What are you?

KAYAMA: I am Prefect of Police for the city of Uraga and I demand that you—

SECOND OFFICER *(Breaking in)*: You . . . policeman?

KAYAMA: Yes, the Prefect of—

SECOND OFFICER: You think officers of great Commodore Payry speak with policeman?

(Scary guffaw)

Ha-Ha!

KAYAMA: But I am the representative of the Shogun. I have the authority—

SECOND OFFICER: Americans speak only to great men. Send great man. You hear? Policeman! Ha!

(Nods to First Officer and starts away)

Tell him—off!

FIRST OFFICER *(To Kayama)*: Go!

KAYAMA: But—

FIRST OFFICER: Go!

(Aims gun)

KAYAMA: Ah yes. Excuse me, please. Forgive me.

(He gestures to his Boatman who starts away. All the Sailors roar with laughter. Kayama swings back to them, deeply insulted and humiliated)

Why do they laugh? I do not laugh.

(More laughter. The boat returns to land where the Second and Third Councilors are waiting. Kayama gets out of the boat and prostrates himself before them)

SECOND COUNCILOR: You have ordered them to go away?

THIRD COUNCILOR: You have terrified them with the sacred decree?

KAYAMA: I am ashamed, my lords. They will not listen to me. They say they will only speak with a more important personage.

SECOND COUNCILOR: You told them you were Prefect of Police?

KAYAMA: Yes, my lord, but they only laughed at me. They said:

(Imitating)

Americans speak only to great man. I think they mean—

BOTH COUNCILORS *(Appalled)*: Us?

KAYAMA: Yes, my lords.

BOTH COUNCILORS: Impossible!

KAYAMA: You needn't go yourselves, my lords. How can barbarians know who is important and who is not? They would assume that anyone dressed in a Councilor's robes—

THIRD COUNCILOR: He is right.

SECOND COUNCILOR: But who?

KAYAMA: My lords, since he has knowledge of their ways, if he has not yet been disposed of—perhaps the ship-wrecked fisherman—

SECOND COUNCILOR: There is no shipwrecked fisherman.

KAYAMA: Forgive me, my lords. There was a rumor . . . Be careful as you step in—

(He indicates the boat; a beat)

THIRD COUNCILOR: Summon him at once.

(Two Sumo Wrestlers carry on the cage containing the fisherman Manjiro, and Kayama crosses to it)

KAYAMA: You have been condemned to death for consorting with foreigners.

MANJIRO: Yes, my lord.

KAYAMA: You are fortunate. The Shogunate has given me permission to make use of you.

(To the Sumo Wrestlers)

Release the prisoner.

(The Wrestlers drag Manjiro out of his cage and throw him at Kayama's feet)

MANJIRO: I am free, my lord?

KAYAMA: For the time being.

(Manjiro prostrates himself before Kayama)

MANJIRO: May you live ten times ten thousand years, my lord!

(Kayama grunts impatiently and turns back toward the Councilors. Manjiro pulls at one of the Sumo Wrestlers' obis, undoing the knot, then dashes across to join Kayama)

RECITER: The fisherman Manjiro is abruptly promoted and strategies are discussed.

(To a percussion accompaniment, the Two Councilors and

Manjiro mime a stylized, silent, babbling conference. During it, an Attendant brings in a splendid robe which is put on Manjiro. The conference abruptly stops.

Kayama and Manjiro bow to the Councilors and go to the guard boat)

KAYAMA: Remember, hold yourself with great dignity, and not a word! Sit in the bow.

(Manjiro nods and takes up his position very grandly. Kayama stands behind him as the boat returns to the U.S.S. Powhatan)

KAYAMA *(Calling up to the First Officer)*: Please!
FIRST OFFICER *(Barking)*: What?
KAYAMA: I must speak with your superiors.
FIRST OFFICER: Why?
KAYAMA: I have returned to present to them a very important dignitary. So if you will call them.
FIRST OFFICER: Busy!
KAYAMA: But I see them standing over there. Please—
MANJIRO *(Breaking in suddenly, with tremendous authority)*: Idiot! How dare you plead with petty officers in *my* presence.

(Gesturing to the Officers)

You! Here! Come here!

(Kayama gives him a look of appalled horror. From the corner of his mouth, to Kayama)

Don't worry. I know how to handle Americans.

(Shouting at Officers)

Man, you hear me. Come, I say.

(For a beat the Officers are bewildered, hesitate, then come down to the rail. Imperiously to Kayama)

Tell these . . . persons who I am.

KAYAMA *(Bowing to him)*: Oh yes, my lord.

(To Officers)

This is the great Councilor, Lord Manjiro, second in power only to the Shogun himself.

MANJIRO *(To Officers)*: Do barbarians not bow to their superiors?

(An uncertain glance between the Officers, who then give a small bow)

That is better.

(Gesturing towards Perry)

Now . . . who is your leader?

SECOND OFFICER: Matthew Calbraith Payry . . . er . . . sir. Commodore. U.S. Navy.

MANJIRO: Tell him to come here.

OFFICERS *(Astounded)*: Tell him?

MANJIRO: Here. To confer with me!

(The Two Officers look uneasily at Perry, who turns majestically away)

SECOND OFFICER: Impossible, sorry. You confer us. We confer Commodore Payry.

MANJIRO: I confer *only* with this Payry.

KAYAMA *(Shocked by this daring, tugging at his sleeve)*: But, my lord—

(Whispers in his ear)

MANJIRO *(Impatiently)*: Very well. For the sake of courtesy, I will make a great concession.

(Indicating Perry)

He confers with you—

(To Officers)

You confer with *him*—

(Indicating Kayama)

He confers with *me*.

(To Kayama)

Ask them why they are here.

KAYAMA: Why are you here?

SECOND OFFICER: We bring greetings and friendly letter from our great President Millyard Fillmore.

MANJIRO: Tell them: Give me the letter and return to America.

KAYAMA: Give the letter to my lord Manjiro, and return to America.

(The Officers go into a very brief, stylized babble conference)

SECOND OFFICER: Impossible. Letter given only to Emperor.

KAYAMA *(Appalled)*: Emperor!

SECOND OFFICER: Or if against religion, to Shogun.

KAYAMA: Shogun!

SECOND OFFICER: In six days time, you prepare big ceremony. Commodore Payry bring letter. Shogun receive it. Much talk and gifts.

FIRST OFFICER: Six days time. Big ceremony.

(Pointing to land)

There!

KAYAMA: But that is impossible! There is a decree, sacred for centuries, which forbids—

MANJIRO *(Breaking in)*: You do not land here. No barbarian sets foot on shore here. You go and tell that to your Payry. Go, I say. Go tell your Payry: All landing— forbidden. Go.

(The Officers hesitate)

On the double!

(The Officers scurry off to confer with Perry)

How'm I doing?

KAYAMA: They seem to be impressed.

MANJIRO: Americans are easy. They shout. You shout louder.

(Their conference with Perry concluded, the Officers come striding back to the rail)

SECOND OFFICER: You want hear great Commodore Payry's reply to you?

MANJIRO: I will listen.

SECOND OFFICER: Commodore Payry say: Much honored by visit of Japanese Lord. Sends warm greetings.

MANJIRO: I accept his greetings.

SECOND OFFICER: Commodore Payry say: Not to worry. All Japanese customs will be respected in all possible ways.

MANJIRO *(To Kayama)*: Didn't I tell you?

SECOND OFFICER: Commodore Payry also say: If big arrangement not made to greet him on land, he turn all cannon on Uraga and blast it off face of earth!!

(There is a roar of laughter from the Americans, as Kayama and Manjiro fall back in their boat, terrified)

SCENE 5

RECITER: Disaster! The Americans insist upon landing. The court of the Shogun is in an uproar. How shall this barbarian threat be frustrated? The Shogun himself, as is his custom when confronted by emergencies, has gathered about him his most trusted advisors, and taken to his bed. And now, at long last, the Shogun! And his wife—

(As the Reciter introduces each character, that character makes an entrance down the hanamichi into the Shogun's chamber)

his physician, his priests, his soothsayer, his sumo wrestlers, his companion—and his mother. The Shogun!

(The Reciter throws off his Reciter's robes and himself becomes the Shogun. He begins rapidly eating rice, grunting. Occasionally, he swills sake. He looks over the rim of the bowl with beady, suspicious eyes at the rest of the room.

His Wife plays the koto and sings, to no one's pleasure. His Mother sits calmly, slowly fanning. A Physician brews tea. Two Priests, Two Sumo Wrestlers, a Samurai Companion and a Soothsayer complete the court)

WIFE *(Sings)*:
   Ahhhhhhh . . .

MOTHER *(Sings)*:
   My lord . . .

   (He pays no attention)

WIFE:
   Ahhhhhhh . . .

MOTHER:
   My lord . . .

WIFE:
   Ahhhhhhh . . .

MOTHER *(Loud)*: *Noble* lord . . .

(He stops eating, startled, looks at her)
WIFE:
> Ahhhhhhh . . .

(The Shogun gestures her to be quiet)

MOTHER:
> It's the Day of the Rat, my lord.
> There are four days remaining,
> And I see you're entertaining,
> But we should have a chat, my lord.
>
> To begin, if I may, my lord,
> I've no wish to remind you
> But you'll notice just behind you
> There are ships in the bay,
> They've been sitting there all day
> With a letter to convey
> And they haven't gone away
> And there's every indication
> That they're planning to stay, my lord . . .
> My lord . . .

(He looks behind him; the ships glow faintly; he stares, transfixed. He looks at her in alarm; she gestures to the Physician to bring the tea)

> Have some tea, my lord,
> Some chrysanthemum tea.
> It's an herb that's superb
> For disturbances at sea.

(The Shogun makes a face at the taste)

> Is the Shogun feeling better?
> Good! Now what about this letter?
> Is it wise to delay, my lord?

With the days disappearing,
Might we benefit from hearing
What the soothsayers say, my lord? . . .

(Physician gets tea from Shogun)

My lord . . . venerable lord . . .

(Shogun gestures to Soothsayer)

SOOTHSAYER *(Comes forward, incants)*:
Ahhhhhhh . . .

(Unrolls an astrological chart)

Wood star . . .
Water star . . .
All celestial omens are—

(The Court holds its breath as he checks)

Excellent.

(They sigh with relief; he casts an I Ching*)*

Deerbones . . .
Turtleshells . . .
Each configuration spells—

(They hold their breath again)

Victory.

(They sigh)

Ahhhhhhh—

(Whirling and pointing up)

A spider on the wall!

(Wife shrieks, Court is alarmed)

Signifies success.

(They relax)

Whose success I cannot guess . . .

(Attempting to recover quickly, as the Shogun grunts disapproval)

Unless . . .

(He looks intently at the chart, desperately trying to bluff his way out of the blunder.

The ships glow ominously as all turn to see them; the Shogun gestures imperiously to the Sumo Wrestlers, who cart the Soothsayer away; all change position; the Festival Drum sounds; a New Day begins.

The Shogun is drawing deeply on a pipe filled with opium)

WIFE:
>Ahhhhhhh . . .
>Ahhhhhhh . . .

MOTHER:
>It's the Day of the Ox, my lord.

(Wife sings right through her; since the Shogun doesn't stop her—he's too stoned to hear her—the Mother does)

>With but three days remaining
>And today already waning,
>I've a few further shocks, my lord.

(Shogun gives pipe back to Samurai)

>To begin, let me say,
>At the risk of repetition,
>There are ships in the bay,
>And they didn't ask permission,
>But they sit there all day

In contemptuous array
With a letter to convey
And they haven't gone away
And there's every indication
That they still plan to stay,
And you look a little gray, my lord . . .
My lord . . .

Have some tea, my lord,
Some chrysanthemum tea,
While we plan, if we can,
What our answer ought to be.
If the tea the Shogun drank will
Serve to keep the Shogun tranquil,
I suggest, if I may, my lord,
We consult the Confucians—
They have mystical solutions.
There are none wise as they, my lord . . .

(The Shogun has difficulty focusing)

Over there, my lord . . .

PRIESTS *(Sing)*:
Night waters do not break the moon.
That merely is illusion.
The moon is sacred.

No foreign ships can break our laws.
That also is illusion.
Our laws are sacred.

It follows there can be no ships.
They must be an illusion.
Japan is sacred.

(Everybody has nodded throughout; they look hopefully out at the bay; the ships glow; the Shogun gestures furiously to the Sumo Wrestlers; the Priests are taken away; Festival Drum; a New Day)

WIFE:
   Ahhhhhhh . . .

   (Her song is sadder, though no less irritating)

   Ahhhhhhh . . .

   (The Shogun gestures at her weakly to stop)

MOTHER:
   It's the Day of the Tiger, my lord.
   Only two days remaining,
   And I'm tired of explaining
   There are ships in the bay
   With a letter to convey,
   They're on permanent display,
   And we must take some position
   Or the Southern Coalition
   Will be soon holding sway, my lord . . .
   And we'll all have to pay, my lord . . .

   (Shogun gestures weakly)

   Have you something to say, my lord?

   (Physician crosses to Shogun)

   Have some tea, my lord,
   Some chrysanthemum tea.
   It's a tangled situation,
   As your father would agree.
   And it mightn't be so tangled
   If you hadn't had him strangled—
   But I fear that I stray, my lord.
   I've a nagging suspicion
   That, in view of your condition,
   What we should do is pray, my lord . . .

   (The Shogun tries weakly to turn away)

   What we should do is pray, my lord.

(He nods, beaten; the Samurai Companion starts the prayer)

SAMURAI COMPANION *(Sings)*:
Blow, wind.
Great wind.
Great Kamikaze,
Winds of the gods.

SAMURAI, SUMO WRESTLERS, PHYSICIAN:
Blow, wind!
Smite them down!
Make the invaders dance and drown!

SAMURAI, SUMO WRESTLERS, PHYSICIAN, WIFE,
MOTHER:
Blow, wind!
Build the waves!
Hurl the infection
Out of the ocean,
Blow, wind!
Blow, wind!
Blow, wind!

(They wait for a moment, then look out at the bay; the ship glows; the Samurai leaves; the New Day)

WIFE:
Ahhhhhhh . . .

MOTHER:
It's the Day of the Rabbit, my lord.
There's but one day remaining,
And beside the fact it's raining,
There are ships in the bay
Which are sitting there today
Just exactly where they sat
On the Day of the Rat—

Oh, and speaking of that, my lord . . .

(Shogun drops)

My lord—?

(Shogun dies)

PHYSICIAN *(Pulling a blanket up over the Shogun's head)*:
The blossom falls on the mountain.
The mountain falls on the blossom.
All things fall—

(Shogun twitches)

Sometimes.

(The Shogun feebly brings his head out from under the blanket; as soon as his Mother sees his eyes, she resumes)

MOTHER:
As I started to say:
From that first disturbing day,
When I gave consideration
To this letter they convey,
I decided if there weren't
Any Shogun to receive it,
It would act as a deterrent
Since they'd have no place to leave it,
And they might go away, my lord . . .
Do you see what I say, my lord?
My Lord?

(The Physician offers tea to the Shogun, who pushes it away as he realizes what it is; his Mother nods)

In the tea, my lord,
The chrysanthemum tea—
An informal variation
On the normal recipe.

Though I know my plan had merit,
It's been slow in execution.
If there's one thing you inherit,
It's your father's constitution,
And you're taking so long, my lord . . .

(As he sinks)

Do you think I was wrong, my lord? . . .

(He tries to say something)

No, you must let me speak:
When the Shogun is weak,
Then the tea must be strong, my lord . . .

(He falls back)

My Lord—?

(He dies. The Physician sings with the Mother)

The blossom falls on the mountain.
The mountain falls on the blossom.
All things—

(She checks the body)

Fall.

(The ships glow again; the Mother looks at them, smiles and fans; the Sumo Wrestlers and the Physician and the Wife clear the stage)

SCENE 6

A tableau: Kayama and Manjiro on their knees. On one side, a Samurai standing guard over them. On the other,

*an enormous Sumo Wrestler honing a sword on a stone
wheel. Upstage of them, posed formally on a low
platform, Lord Abe and the Third Councilor.*

ABE: The Americans have not left!

KAYAMA: No, my lord.

ABE: But they have agreed to leave?

KAYAMA: No, my lord.

ABE: Then you have failed completely!

KAYAMA: Yes, my lord—no my lord. My lord, forgive me,
but arrangements must be made for the Americans to
land and deliver a letter from their President.

ABE: Land!

THIRD COUNCILOR: You told them they could come
ashore!

ABE: Kill them!

(The Sumo Wrestler gleefully grinds his sword)

KAYAMA: Please, my lord, if you will permit me to
explain—I have a plan!

ABE: Explain.

KAYAMA: My lord, no power on earth can prevent the
Americans from landing. But if they were to come
ashore—at Kanagawa.

THIRD COUNCILOR *(Astonished)*: Kanagawa?

ABE: The sacred decree is most specific. It forbids any
foreigners to set foot on our soil.

KAYAMA: That is why I suggested Kanagawa, my lord.
The cove there is quite small. It occurred to me that we
could cover all the sand with mats—tatami mats—and
build a special treaty house, to receive the letter with
courtesy, and many heartfelt promises of a reply.

THIRD COUNCILOR: What does he mean?

ABE *(Silencing him)*: And then?

(The Sumo Wrestler grinds his sword)

KAYAMA: And then? And then—

(A glance at Manjiro)

When the Westerners are satisfied and have departed, we destroy the house and burn the mats and, my lord, neither the decree nor our honor will have been betrayed. The Americans will have come and gone, without setting foot on our sacred soil.

(For a long moment Abe merely stares at him. Then he bursts into laughter. He gestures to the Sumo Wrestler, who reluctantly puts aside his sword)

ABE: Brilliant! Magnificent! Kayama Yesaemon, you will make all necessary arrangements to receive them—as the new *Governor* of the City of Uraga.

KAYAMA: My lord, how can I prove worthy of so great an honor. And yet, dare I ask. . . ?

ABE: Another favor?

KAYAMA: The fisherman Manjiro has been most helpful to me. My lord, if it were possible to revoke his death sentence and attach him to my service—

ABE: He is yours.

(The Court starts to move off)

RECITER: If the Councilors can no longer pretend that the Americans are not coming, they have not yet given up the hope of pretending the Americans were never here.

MANJIRO: My Lord Governor of Uraga, you have saved my life.

KAYAMA: And why not, my friend, when you saved mine. The mats were your idea.

MANJIRO: You, a samurai, calling me, a fisherman— friend! This is not Japan. This is America.

KAYAMA: America?

MANJIRO: It is not the Americans who are barbarians. It is us! If you could have seen what I have seen in America—

(Pause)

But what I feel in my heart is enough to have me boiled in oil.

KAYAMA: I think you are going to be far too useful to me to boil. But now I must return to Uraga. My wife has had no word from me for many days, and will be worried. Come with me. It is a long journey and we can keep each other company.

(Kayama and Manjiro start the walk to Uraga, "in place," with underscoring)

I will make a poem.

(Sings)

Rain glistening
On the silver birch,
Like my lady's tears.
Your turn.

MANJIRO *(Sings)*:
Rain gathering,
Winding into streams,
Like the roads to Boston.
Your turn.

KAYAMA:
Haze hovering,
Like the whisper of the silk
As my lady kneels.
Your turn.

MANJIRO:
Haze glittering,

Like an echo of the lamps
In the streets of Boston.
Your turn.

KAYAMA:

Moon,
I love her like the moon,
Making jewels of the grass
Where my lady walks,
My lady wife.

MANJIRO:

Moon,
I love her like the moon,
Washing yesterday away,
As my lady does—
America.
Your turn.

KAYAMA:

Wind murmuring.
Is she murmuring for me
Through her field of dreams?
Your turn.

MANJIRO:

Wind muttering.
Is she quarreling with me?
Does she want me home?
Your turn.

KAYAMA:

I am no nightingale,
But she hears the song
I can sing to her,
My lady wife.

MANJIRO:
> I am no nightingale,
> But my song of her
> Could outsing the sea—
> America.

KAYAMA:
> Dawn flickering,
> Tracing shadows of the pines
> On my lady sleeping.
> Your turn.

MANJIRO:
> Dawn brightening
> As she opens up her eyes,
> But it's I who come awake.
> Your turn.

> *(Pause)*

KAYAMA:
> You go.

> *(Pause)*

MANJIRO:
> Your turn.

> *(Pause)*

BOTH:
> Leaves,
> I love her like the leaves,
> Changing green to pink to gold,
> And the change is everything.
> Sun,
> I see her like the sun
> In the center of a pool,

Sending ripples to the shore,
Till my journey's end.

(Kayama's house appears)

MANJIRO:
Your turn.

KAYAMA:
Rain.

MANJIRO:
Haze.

KAYAMA:
Moon.

MANJIRO:
Wind.

KAYAMA:
Nightingale.

MANJIRO:
Dawn.

KAYAMA:
Leaves.

MANJIRO:
Sun.

BOTH:
End.

KAYAMA *(Arriving at his house; to Manjiro)*: Wait here.

(He enters the house and approaches Tamate, who is turned away from him, kneeling at the household shrine)

Tamate, I have the most extraordinary things to tell you! I have been to Edo and appeared before

the Councilors. You won't believe what happened. I
was—

*(In his excitement Kayama has not noticed that Tamate
hasn't moved.*

*Downstage and below, Manjiro waits impatiently, his
attention elsewhere.*

The Reciter watches the scene)

Tamate?

(He walks slowly up behind her and reaches out)

Tamate. What is it?

(Kayama puts his hand on Tamate's shoulder.

*She falls into his arms. He appears to cry out, silently.
The appropriate sound comes from the Reciter. Kayama
turns her gently around. She is clutching one of his short
swords in her hands, the front of her robes soaked in
blood. He falls to his knees, letting her body gently to the
ground. There is what seems to be an endless pause, filled
only with the wracked sobbing of the Reciter)*

MANJIRO *(Impatiently, from outside)*: Kayama!

(The Reciter's sobbing continues)

KAYAMA *(Woodenly)*: A moment.

*(Kayama rises from the floor, moving Downstage.
Noticing the blood on his hands, mechanically, he wipes
them clean.*

The Reciter, still sobbing.

*Kayama joins Manjiro, who is too excited to notice the
change in his friend. He leads him away from the house,
up the hanamichi)*

MANJIRO: What did she say?

(No response from Kayama)

Oh, she's probably just as terrified of the Americans as all the rest of you. But she'll see, you'll all see. Their coming here is the best thing that ever happened to Japan!

(As Manjiro and Kayama make their way up the hanamichi, they are passed by a garish, middle-aged Madam coming down)

SCENE 7

The Madam looks impatiently back over her shoulder at Four Girls who are following her, with some reluctance, down toward the stage.

MADAM: Hurry up, girls, for goodness' sake. The Americans will have already landed.

(Sings, to the audience)

I own a small commercial venture
With a modest clientele
In Kanagawa.

GIRLS *(Sing, in tandem)*:
I think I see one over there behind the trees!

MADAM:
Sh!

(To the audience)

It's been my family's for centuries
And doing very well—
For Kanagawa.

GIRLS *(In tandem)*:
I hear they're covered all with hair, like some disease.

MADAM:
Sh!

GIRLS:
Except their knees.

MADAM:
Sh!

(To the audience)

The arrival of these giants
Out of the blue,
Bringing panic to my clients,
Alters my view.
With so many of them fleeing,
Conferring, decreeing,
I find myself agreeing
With the ancient haiku:

RECITER:
The nest-building bird,
Seeing the tree without twigs,
Looks for new forests.

MADAM: Exactly.

(A "forest" of bamboo poles, carried on by Stagehands, forms on stage. The Madam searches through it)

Yo-ho! Americans!

GIRLS *(Also searching)*:
Yo-ho! Americans!

MADAM:
Welcome to Kanagawa.

GIRLS *(Raucously)*:
> Welcome to Kanagawa!

MADAM:
> No . . .

> *(Delicately)*

> Welcome to Kanagawa.

GIRLS:
> Oh . . .

> *(Imitating)*

> Welcome to Kanagawa.

MADAM:
> So . . .

> *(As the Girls continue singing softly)*

> With all my flowers disappearing
> In alarm,
> I've been reduced to commandeering
> From the farm.

> *(Shrugs)*

> But with appropriate veneering,
> Even green wood has its charm.

GIRLS *(Searching)*:
> Yo-ho!
> Yo-ho!

MADAM *(Beckoning them)*:
> Yo-ho!

> *(The Madam hands out pornographic fans to the Girls and points to each in turn)*

> That you do lightly,
> Just with your toes . . .

FIRST GIRL:
Yo-ho!

MADAM:
That you hold tightly
When you're toying with

(Pointing)

Those . . .

SECOND GIRL:
Yo-ho!

MADAM *(To Third Girl, who is holding her fan sideways)*:
This you do through the kimono—
Go and rehearse . . .

THIRD GIRL:
Yo-ho!

MADAM *(To Fourth Girl)*:
This will take two of you—

(To the Third Girl, who has turned her fan upside down)

No no no no,
Just the reverse!

ALL:
Welcome to Kanagawa,
Music and food for twenty yen—
Music and food—

MADAM:
And maybe then—

ALL:
Welcome!

GIRLS:
Welcome to Kanagawa!

MADAM:
>Low . . .

GIRLS *(Lowering their voices)*:
>Welcome to Kanagawa.

MADAM:
>So . . .

>*(The Girls continue singing underneath)*

>You must neither be too wary
>Nor too bold,
>As there's no telling with barbarians,
>I'm told,
>Because not only are they hairy,
>But extremely uncontrolled.

GIRLS *(Excited)*:
>Yo-ho!

MADAM *(Beckoning them)*:
>Yo-ho!

>*(To First Girl, pointing to fan)*

>That you mustn't wash for,
>Not till you're done.

FIRST GIRL:
>Yo-ho!

MADAM *(To Second Girl, similarly)*:
>That you use a squash for—
>Or pumpkins are fun.

SECOND GIRL:
>Yo-ho!

MADAM *(To Third Girl)*:
>That you do slow-

Ly and gently—
Don't take a chance.

THIRD GIRL:
Yo-ho!

MADAM *(To Fourth Girl)*:
That they don't know
About, evidently—
Get an advance.

ALL:
Welcome to Kanagawa!
Music and food—

MADAM:
—for twenty yen!

ALL:
Music and food—

MADAM:
—or even ten—

ALL:
Welcome!

(Dance)

MADAM:
When a country is in trouble,
Choices are few.
And apart from charging double,
What can you do?
With my clients off defending,
And strangers descending,
I find myself depending
On the ancient haiku:

RECITER:
The bird from the sea,

Not knowing pine from bamboo,
Roosts on anything.

MADAM:
Exactly.

(Dance)

MADAM *(Furiously, to the Fourth Girl, who dropped her fan)*:
Back to the farm!

(Girl starts off disconsolately; Madam stops her)

Tomorrow!

(Dance)

GIRLS:
Welcome to Kanagawa!

MADAM:
Flow!

GIRLS *(Flowing)*: Welcome to Kanagawa!

MADAM:
Glow!

GIRLS *(Glowing)*: Welcome to Kanagawa!

MADAM:
Grow!

GIRLS *(Loudly)*: Welcome to Kanagawa!

MADAM *(Like a general to her troops)*:
Go!

GIRLS:
Welcome to Kanagawa! Yo-ho!
Welcome to Kanagawa! Yo-ho!

(Repeated, until first the Girls and then the Madam have exited)

SCENE 8

A Samurai enters holding up to his face an Old Man's mask.

SAMURAI: The Americans insisted that their mission was a peaceful one. But because we did not know if we could trust them, we chose a samurai whose task it was to muster our defenses. And that samurai . . .

(Dropping the mask and emerging as a Younger Man)

—was me. I ordered canvas screens to be stretched across the cliffs at Kanagawa.

(Stagehands enter with a strip of canvas which indicates the screens)

Behind the screens, I was able to conceal—five thousand armored swordsmen—

(Below the screen appear the legs of the Swordsmen)

—carrying enormous bows—

(The tips of the bows appear above the screen)

—all of them on horseback!

(The legs disappear and are replaced by hooves)

A most impressive force—and with the canvas masking them our enemy might think that twice, three times that many warriors were assembled. At least that's what we thought. But when the Americans saw our screens they called out from the ships. "Pull down those drapes. What kind of army hides behind a parlor curtain!" And then—they roared with laughter.

(He draws his sword in frustration, then slams it back in its sheath)

Most discouraging. I mean, what are you going to do with people like that?

(The Samurai bows and exits, raising the Old Man's mask back up to his face and chanting his opening lines.

The screen follows him)

SCENE 9

RECITER: From the personal journal of Commodore Matthew Calbraith Perry. 14 July, 1853. As I supervise the final preparations for this afternoon's historic landing at Kanagawa, I am moved to hope the Japanese will voluntarily accept the reasonable and pacific overtures embodied in our friendly letter. Should I hope in vain, however, should these backward, semibarbarous people be reluctant to forsake their policy of isolation, then I stand prepared to introduce them into the community of civilized nations by whatever means are necessary. It is my understanding that this preposterous empire has been closed to foreigners for over two hundred and fifty years, and I for one feel that that has been more than long enough!

(The Treaty House at Kanagawa is assembled Onstage. Festive kites are lowered from the flies, a tree is rolled on — the stage is set for the Americans' arrival. Abe, the Second Councilor, Kayama and several Samurai emerge from the house and stare up the hanamichi)

ABE: They are late. It is an insult.

SECOND COUNCILOR: Where is the warrior?

KAYAMA: Here, my lord!

Kayama slides back a panel in the base of the house, revealing a Samurai hidden under the floorboards)

ABE: He understands the signal?

KAYAMA: Yes, my lord. If the Westerners should draw their weapons, I will knock twice and he will come up through the floor and cut them down.

SECOND COUNCILOR: Pity the Americans if they should draw their guns.

(The sound of an American march from the rear of the hanamichi)

They come!

ABE: Inside!

(Abe and the Second Councilor disappear inside the Treaty House. Simultaneously, a Samurai appears at the rear of the hanamichi, rolling straw matting down toward the stage. The sound of American marching music is heard, as behind him comes the American landing party: a marching band, a row of Enlisted Men, the Two American Officers, and finally Perry himself. The Enlisted Men form ranks outside the house, while Perry and the Officers are escorted inside)

RECITER: No one knows what was said behind the shutters of the Treaty House. The Shogun's Councilors kept their story secret, and though the Westerners have their own official version—I would not believe a word of it. What a shame that there is no authentic Japanese account of what took place on that historic day.

(An Old Japanese Man carrying an attaché case enters. Music changes)

OLD MAN *(Sings)*:
> Pardon me, I was there.

RECITER *(Sings)*:
> You were where?

OLD MAN:
> At the Treaty House.

RECITER:
> At the Treaty House?

OLD MAN:
> There was a tree . . .

RECITER:
> Which was where?

OLD MAN:
> Very near.

RECITER *(Indicating)*:
> Over here?

OLD MAN *(Indicating)*:
> Maybe over there,
> But there were trees then, everywhere.
> May I show you?

RECITER:
> If you please.

OLD MAN:
> There were trees
> Then, everywhere . . .

RECITER:
> But you were there.

OLD MAN:
> And I was there!

Let me show you.

RECITER:

If you please.

OLD MAN:

I was younger then . . .

(Tries to climb; defensively)

I was good at climbing trees . . .

(Tries again; apologetically)

I was younger then . . .

(Again)

I saw everything.
I was hidden all the time . . .

(Again)

It was easier to climb . . .

(Again)

I was younger then.

(Again)

I saw everything!

(Again)

Where they came and where they went—
I was part of the event.
I was someone in a tree.

(Again, now desperate)

I was younger then!

(Suddenly a Young Boy appears, scurries across stage and up the tree)

BOY *(Triumphantly, to the Old Man)*:
 Tell him what I see!

OLD MAN *(To Reciter)*:
 I am in a tree.
 I am ten.
 I am in a tree.

BOY *(Sings, to Reciter)*:
 I was younger then.

OLD MAN:
 In between the eaves I can see—

 (To Boy)

 Tell me what I see.

 (To Reciter)

 I was only ten.

BOY *(Peering into the Treaty House)*:
 I see men and matting.
 Some are old, some chatting.

OLD MAN:
 If it happened, I was there!

BOTH:
 I saw (see) everything!

OLD MAN:
 I was someone in a tree.

BOY:
 Tell him what I see.

OLD MAN:
 Some of them have gold on their coats.

BOY *(Correcting him)*:
 One of them has gold.

(To the Reciter)

He was younger then.

OLD MAN:
Someone crawls around, passing notes—

BOY:
Someone very old—

OLD MAN *(To the Reciter)*:
He was only ten.

BOY:
And there's someone in a tree—

OLD MAN:
—or the day is incomplete.

BOTH:
Without someone in a tree,
Nothing happened here.

OLD MAN:
I am hiding in a tree.

BOY:
I'm a fragment of the day.

BOTH:
If I weren't, who's to say
Things would happen here the way
That they happened here?

OLD MAN:
I was there then.

BOY:
It's the fragment, not the day.
I am here still.

OLD MAN:
It's the pebble, not the stream.

BOTH:

>It's the ripple, not the sea,
>Not the building but the beam,
>Not the garden but the stone,
>Not the Treaty House,
>Someone in a tree.

WARRIOR *(Slides panel open underneath the house, sings)*:

>Pardon me, I am here.
>If you please, I am also here—

(The others pay no attention)

OLD MAN:

>I could see between the eaves.

RECITER:

>Yet you say you weren't seen.

OLD MAN:

>I remember, there were leaves . . .

BOY:

>It was summer, they were green . . .

(The tree sprouts leaves)

WARRIOR:

>If you please, I am here.

RECITER *(Noticing)*:

>You are where?

WARRIOR:

>In the Treaty House.

RECITER:

>In the Treaty House?

WARRIOR:

>Or very near.

RECITER:

Can you hear?

WARRIOR:

I'm below.

RECITER:

So I notice.

WARRIOR:

Underneath the floor,
And so I can't see anything.
I can hear them,
But I can't see anything.

RECITER:

But you can hear?

WARRIOR:

But I can hear.
Shall I listen?

RECITER:

If you please.

WARRIOR:

I can hear them now . . .

(Pressing his ear closer)

I shall try to shift my knees . . .

(He does)

I can hear them now . . .

(Obviously not hearing)

I hear everything!
I'm the part that's underneath,
With my sword inside my sheath.

(Listening again)

I can hear them now . . .

(Again)

One is over me.
If they knock, then I appear!
I'm a part of what I hear!
I'm the fragment underneath!

(Listening, triumphantly)

I can hear them now!

RECITER, OLD MAN, BOY:
Tell us what you hear!

WARRIOR:
First I hear a creak and a thump.
Now I hear a clink . . .
Then they talk a bit . . .
Many times they shout when they speak.
Other times they think.
Or they argue it . . .
I hear floorboards groaning . . .
Angry growls . . . much droning . . .
Since I hear them, they are there!
As they argue it,
I'm the listener underneath.

BOY *(Peering into the House)*:
Someone reads a list
From a box . . .

WARRIOR *(Listening)*:
Someone talks of laws . . .

OLD MAN:
Then they fan a bit . . .

BOY:
Someone bangs a fist . . .

WARRIOR:
Someone knocks . . .

OLD MAN:
Now there was a pause.

ALL:
Then they argue it:

WARRIOR:
"But we want . . ."
"No, you can't and we won't . . ."
"But we need it and we want . . ."
"Will you grant—? . . . If you don't . . ."
"We concede it . . ."

OLD MAN:	WARRIOR:	BOY:
And they sat Through the night And they lit Yellow tapers.	I can hear them.	
I was There Then.	I'm a Fragment of the Day.	And they Chat And they fight And they sit, Signing papers.
If I Weren't, who's to Say Things would Happen here the Way That they're Happening?	If I Weren't, who's to Say Things would Happen here the Way That they're Happening?	I am There Still. If I Weren't, who's to Say That they're Happening?

ALL:
It's the fragment, not the day.

It's the pebble, not the stream.
It's the ripple, not the sea
That is happening.
Not the building but the beam,
Not the garden but the stone,
Only cups of tea
And history
And someone in a tree!

(The Warrior slides his panel closed. The Old Man and Boy exit)

RECITER: Whatever happened behind the shutters of the Treaty House, Kayama Yesaemon's plan was a success. The letter was delivered. The Americans were satisfied. And they left.

(The American Officers emerge from the House, followed by Abe and his Retainers. Bows are exchanged, then the Officers lead the American Enlisted Men back up the hanamichi)

ABE *(To his Retainers)*: Quickly there, nothing must remain!

(The Treaty House is dismantled, and the stage is cleared)

RECITER: We tore down the house and rolled up the mats, taking great care that the contaminated side should not touch the ground. Once again, all was as it had been. The barbarian threat had forever been removed. Ha!

SCENE 10

Suddenly the lion-like figure of Commodore Perry leaps out Onstage and performs a strutting, leaping dance of triumph which is a combination of the traditional Kabuki lion dance and an American cake walk.

He exits up the hanamichi, waving two small American flags.

ACT II

Tony Marino and Thomas Ikeda in the Off Broadway revival.

SCENE 1

The Reciter enters and kneels at the side of the stage. A
Musician plays the shamisen and sings. A Stagehand
runs the show curtain across the stage, revealing the
Imperial Court in Kyoto—the puppet/Emperor, a Priest,
and two bored Nobles playing cat's cradle.

RECITER: The spiritual heart of all Japan—the court of
the Emperor at Kyoto, the palace of the living god
descended from the sun itself, the throne room of the
sacred ruler of the Islands of Nippon!

(The Priest unfurls a roll of rice paper covered with
calligraphy. Lord Abe and the Councilors enter, followed
by Kayama and Manjiro)

Of course, a thousand years ago the Emperor's
power was wrested from him by the warlord called
the Shogun, and since that time the Emperor has
ruled in name alone. But ancient duties still must
be discharged. Observe how low Lord Abe bows
down to the ruler whom he rules.

(Abe prostrates himself before the puppet/Emperor. The
Priest picks up the sticks which manipulate the puppet's
arms and holds them out. The Nobles pause in their game
and listen)

His holiness the Emperor speaks.

PRIEST *(Speaking for the Emperor, manipulating the puppet's*
arms): The Americans did not come. Had the Americans come, the honor of Japan and the sanctity of its
ancestral soil would have been defiled. But the Ameri-

cans did not come. Therefore . . . the Emperor formally acknowledges Lord Abe Masahiro as the thirteenth Tokugawa Shogun of the Empire of Japan.

(Abe bows curtly)

The Emperor formally acknowledges Kayama Yesaemon as Governor of the city of Uraga.

(Kayama bows curtly)

The Emperor formally rescinds the sentence of death imposed upon the fisherman Manjiro—

(Manjiro bows curtly)

And elevates him to the rank of samurai.

(Manjiro snaps his head up in surprise, then quickly lowers it again. Attendants enter, carrying robes and swords. They raise Manjiro off the floor and drape him in a robe which bears his new family crest. Next the Attendants produce two swords and strap them around Manjiro's waist. With great ceremony they proceed to shave his shaggy wig, leaving only a samurai's topknot at the back. For a moment Manjiro stands transfixed, then he falls back to his knees and prostrates himself before the Emperor)

PRIEST *(Grandly)*: The Emperor congratulates the saviors of Japan—

(Abe, the Councilors, Kayama and Manjiro bow)

And respectfully suggests that his monthly allowance of incense is inadequate.

FIRST NOBLE: The Emperor respectfully suggests that his monthly allowance of ink is inadequate.

SECOND NOBLE: The Emperor respectfully suggests that his monthly allowance of silk is inadequate.

ABE: As the Emperor knows, there are many even more

important claims on our resources. But the Shogunate will certainly consider any reasonable requests.

RECITER: A haiku:
The hand which feeds it grudgingly
Is the first hand
Which the dog will bite.

(He smiles)

If it ever gets the chance.

PRIEST *(Speaking for the Emperor)*: The Emperor smiles on his loyal subjects and permits them to depart—secure in the knowledge that the barbarian threat has forever been removed.

(Lord Abe backs out of the Court and is isolated from it by a curtain which drops behind his back)

ABE: Goodbye America. Come back in another two hundred fifty years!

(He laughs)

SCENE 2

Abe is surprised by the sudden sound of a marching band. An American Admiral enters down the hanamichi, carrying a plaque and some official documents.

AMERICAN ADMIRAL *(Sings, to Abe)*:
Please hello, America back,
Commodore Perry say hello!
Also comes memorial plaque
President Fillmore wish bestow.

Emperor read our letter? If no,

Commodore Perry very sad.
Emperor like our letter? If so,
Commodore Perry very merry,
President Fillmore still more glad.

Last time we visit, too short.
This time we visit for slow.
Last time we come, come with warships,
Now with more ships—
Say hello!
This time request use of port,
Port for commercial intention,
Harbor with ample dimension.

ABE *(Sings)*:
But you can't—

AMERICAN ADMIRAL:
Only one
Little port
For a freighter.

ABE:
But you can't—

AMERICAN ADMIRAL:
Just for fun.
Be a sport.

ABE:
Maybe later—

AMERICAN ADMIRAL:
But we bring many recent invention:
Kerosene
And cement
And a grain
Elevator,
A machine

You can rent
Called a "train"—

ABE:
    —Maybe later—

AMERICAN ADMIRAL:
    —Also cannon to shoot
Big loud salute,
Like so:

(An explosion offstage. Light flashes. Abe cowers in fear, accepts the document)

Say hello!

(Explosion. Abe takes the pen and signs)

Treaty meet approval? If no,
Commodore Perry very fierce.
Disregard confusion below.
President Fillmore now name Pierce.

(Whisking the paper away and blowing on it to dry the ink)

Good! At last agreement is made,
Letter will let us come again.
First result of mutual trade:
Commodore getting letter letting,

(Gesturing to Abe to keep the pen as a souvenir)

Councilor getting fancy pen!
Goodbye.

(Bows; Abe bows back)

Goodbye.

ABE:
    Goodbye.

(Bows; Admiral bows back)

AMERICAN ADMIRAL:
  Goodbye.

ABE:
  Goodbye.

AMERICAN ADMIRAL:
  Please goodbye.

  (Bows; Abe bows back)

BRITISH ADMIRAL *(Appearing suddenly)*:
  Hello!

AMERICAN ADMIRAL *(To Abe)*:
  Goodbye.

  (Bows; the British Admiral bows in greeting; Abe is confused, bows halfway between them)

BRITISH ADMIRAL:
  Hello, please!

AMERICAN ADMIRAL:
  Goodbye.

  (All three bow again; the American Admiral retires to one side and studies the treaty)

BRITISH ADMIRAL *(In unflappable Gilbert-and-Sullivan style, sings to Abe)*:
  Please
  Hello, I come with letters from Her Majesty Victoria
  Who, learning how you're trading now, sang "Hallelu-
    jah, Gloria!"
  And sent me to convey to you her positive euphoria
  As well as little gifts from Britain's various emporia.

  (Offers a tin of tea to Abe)

RECITER:

> The man has come with letters from Her Majesty Victoria
> As well as little gifts from Britain's various emporia.

ABE:

> Tea?

BRITISH ADMIRAL *(Patiently)*:

> For drink.

ABE:

> I see.
> I thank you—

BRITISH ADMIRAL:

> I think
> Her letters do contain a few proposals to your Emperor
> Which if, of course, he won't endorse, will put her in a temper or,
> More happily, should he agree, will serve to keep her placid, or
> At least till I am followed by a permanent ambassador.

(Waves some documents about)

RECITER:

> A treaty port and, from the Court, a permanent ambassador.
> A treaty port and, from the Court, a permanent ambassador.
> A treaty port and, from the Court, a permanent ambassador.
> And more . . .

BRITISH ADMIRAL:

> Her Majesty considers the arrangements to be tentative

Until we ship a proper diplomatic representative.
We don't foresee that you will be the least bit
argumentative,
So please ignore the man-of-war we brought as a
preventative.

RECITER:
Yes, please ignore the man-of-war
That's anchored rather near to shore.
It's nothing but a metaphor
That acts as a preventative.

*(Another enormous explosion offstage; again light flashes;
again Abe blinks and reaches for the documents)*

BRITISH ADMIRAL:
All clear?
Just so.
Sign here.

(As Abe starts to sign, the American Admiral returns)

AMERICAN ADMIRAL:
Hello, hello, objection, resent!
President Pierce say "moment's pause."
British get ambassador sent,
President Pierce get extra clause.

*(As he presents more papers to Abe, the Dutch Admiral
appears. He is a Dutch comic, Weber-and-Fields style,
complete with Hans Brinker pockets and heavy clogs. He
dances a waltz-clog continually while he sings)*

DUTCH ADMIRAL:
Vait! Please hello!
Don't forget ze Dutch!
Like to keep in touch!
Zank you very much!
Tell zem to go,

Button up ze lips.
Vot do little Nips
Vant vit battleships?

(Dances briefly, withdraws a tulip, waves it enticingly at Abe)

Hold everyzing!
Ve gonna bring
Chocolate!
Vouldn't you like to lease
A beautiful liddle piece
Of chocolate?
Listen, zat's not to mention
Vunderful—pay attention!—
Vindmills
Und tulips,

(Gives Abe the tulip)

Und vouldn' you like a vooden shoe?

(Gives Abe documents)

Zere—can you read?
Good! Ve vill need
Two ports,
Vun of zem not too rocky—
How about Nagasaki?—
Two ports,
Vun of zem for ze cocoa—
Vot do you call it?—Yoko-
Hama! Ja!
Und Nagasaki! Ja!
Sign here!

(Dances, making semaphore signals to the sea.

Another explosion.

The Dutch Admiral settles on the floor in front of Abe, with his back to the audience.

The American and British Admirals cross to Abe.

Simultaneously:)

AMERICAN ADMIRAL:
Wait please, objection again!
Dutch getting too many seaports.
President now wanting *three* ports—

BRITISH ADMIRAL:
Great Britain wishes her position clear and indisput-
able:
We're not amused at being used and therefore stand
immutable.
And though you Japs are foxy chaps and damnably
inscrutable—

*(The Russian Admiral appears at the rear of the
hanamichi. He is very tired and soulful and not terribly
interested in the job at hand; he wears a fancy coat)*

RUSSIAN ADMIRAL *(Sings)*:
Please hello . . .

DUTCH ADMIRAL *(To the other Admirals)*:
Vait! Please hello!
Comes ze monkey wrench!
Smell dot awful stench:
Probably ze French.

AMERICAN ADMIRAL *(Paying no attention, to Abe)*:
—Also insist giving free ports—

BRITISH ADMIRAL *(Ditto, simultaneously)*:
—Reviewing it from where we sit, the facts are
irrefutable—

RUSSIAN ADMIRAL:
Please hello . . .

DUTCH ADMIRAL:
Ach, nein, of course,

78

My mistake, ze Czar.
Smell ze caviar—
Leave ze door ajar.

AMERICAN ADMIRAL *(As above)*:
  —Also want annual Reports—

BRITISH ADMIRAL *(Ditto)*:
  —And thus, in short, a single port is patently unsuitable!

RUSSIAN ADMIRAL *(Loudly)*:
  Please hello,
  Is bringing Czar's request,
  Braving snow
  With letter to protest:
  Since we know
  You trading with the West,
  You might at least

  (As Abe gestures)

  (Don't touch the coat!)
  Start looking East

  (Thinking about it)

  —or closer West—

  (Thinking again)

  —well, farther North—

  (Looking around)

  Are we the fourth?
  I feel depressed.
  (Don't touch the coat!).

  (Pulling himself together unhappily, to Abe, presenting documents. Abe is now inundated)

79

Coming next
Is extraterritoriality.
Noting text
Say "Extraterritoriality."
You perplexed
By "Extraterritoriality"?

(Points)

Just noting clause
(Don't touch the coat!)
Which say your laws
Do not apply
(Don't touch the coat!)
When we drop by—
Not getting shot,
No matter what:
A minor scrape,
A major rape,
And we escape
(Don't touch the cape!)
That's what is extraterritoriality.

(Sighs)

Fair is fair—
You wish perhaps to vote?
What we care
You liking what we wrote?

(Points to sea)

Sitting there
Is finest fleet afloat.
Observing boat?

(Smiles.

Another enormous explosion.

He stands imperturbably, lowering his eyes in silent resignation as Abe instinctively leans forward to cling to him in terror)

Don't touch the coat.

(Another explosion)

Just sign the note.

(As Abe signs, all the other Admirals sing simultaneously, to Abe:)

BRITISH ADMIRAL:

> The British feel these latest dealings verge on immortality.
> The element of precedent imperils our neutrality.
> We're rather vexed, your giving extraterritoriality.
> We must insist you offer this to every nationality!

DUTCH ADMIRAL:

> Ve vant de same
> Vot de Russkies claim!
> Vhy you let them came?
> Dirty rotten shame!

AMERICAN ADMIRAL:

> U.S.A. extremely upset!
> President Pierce say solid "No!"

FRENCH ADMIRAL *(Appears simultaneously—he is a dandy, disgustingly gay and charming)*:
'Allo!—

(No one pays attention)

Please 'allo!

(Again—loudly)

Please 'allo!

(They all look—he smiles broadly)

'Allo! 'Allo! 'Allo!

(Blows them all a kiss and sings)

I bring word, I bring word
From Napoleon ze Third.
'E 'ad 'eard what 'ave occurred
'Ere from ze little bird!
Undeterred, we conferred,
Though we felt zat we'd been slurred,
And ze verdict was he spurred
Me 'ere to bring ze word!
Would you like to know ze word
From Napoleon ze Third?

(Shoves a bundle of papers at Abe)

It's detente! Oui, detente!
Zat's ze only thing we want!
Just detente! Ooh, detente!
No agreements could be more fair!
Signing pacts, passing acts,
Zere's no time for making warfare
When you're always busy making wiz ze
Mutual detente!

(Blows another kiss)

A detente, a detente
Is ze only thing we wish!
Same as zem, except additional
Ze rights to fish!
You'll be paid, you'll be paid,
And we'll 'ave ze big parade
If we somehow can persuade
You to accept our aid.

(Gestures to the sea—

A stylized bass-drum explosion)

It is not to be afraid . . .

(Another one)

As we only wish to trade . . .

(As he smiles to reassure Abe, the biggest explosion yet—it is practically the atom bomb. Abe hastily starts to sign, which causes the others to throw more papers at him)

FRENCH ADMIRAL *(Gaily)*:
  Ah, detente! Oui, detente!
  Zat's ze only thing we want!
  Leave ze grain, leave ze train,
  Put champagne among your imports!
  Tell each man zat Japan
  Can't be bothered giving him ports
  While she's in a tizzy,
  Dizzy wiz ze
  Mutual detente!

ABE *(Pleading to him)*:
  It is late,
  And I fear—
  Well, you see,
  There's a famine . . .
  Could you wait
  For a year?
  We'll agree to
  Examine
  It—

FRENCH ADMIRAL *(Gaily dancing, paying no attention, simultaneously)*:
  A detente! A detente!
  Zat's ze only thing we want!

(And now everybody sings simultaneously)

ABE *(To each in turn)*:
—But lat-
Er, I fear.
There's a drought
And a famine . . .
If you wait
For a year,
Then no doubt
We'll examine
It, but we've
Had a quake
And a flood
And a famine . . .
Please believe
We will take
It to stud-
Y, examine
It, but please,
If you'll wait
For a year . . .
There's a famine . . .

FRENCH ADMIRAL:
Just detente! Oooh,
    detente!
No agreement could be
    more fair!
Signing pacts, passing acts,
Zere's no time for making
    warfare.
Why discuss, make ze fuss,
Since ze West belong to us?
And ze East we have leased
    for ze French
    administration.
If you force in ze Norce,
Zen we burn ze Dutch
    legation.

DUTCH ADMIRAL:
Vait please hallo!
Don't forget ze
    Dutch!
Ve vant just as much
Fishing rights and
    such!
Tell zem to go,
Othervise ve post
Battleships at most
Ports along ze coast.
You can have ze Vest,
Ve vill take ze rest.

BRITISH ADMIRAL:
One moment, please, I
    think that these assure us
    exclusivity
For Western ports and
    other sorts of maritime
    activity,
And if you mean to
    intervene, as is the Dutch
    proclivity,
We'll blow you nits to little
    bits, with suitable
    festivity.

AMERICAN ADMIRAL:

> Wait please, hello, West is ours.
> Wait please, the East is the best coast.
> We'll trade you two on the West coast.

RUSSIAN ADMIRAL:

> Please hello, no seaports on the West.
> United States too near to Czar,
> Is tempting fates, is go too far
> (Don't touch the coat!)

ALL THE ADMIRALS *(Doing the CanCan, to Abe)*:

> Ah, detentes! Ah, detentes!
> They're what everybody wants!
> You should want a detente—
> Makes a nation like a brother!
> We'll be here every year
> To protect you from each other
> And to see you aren't
> Signing foreign
> Treaties and detentes!
> Please hello! We must go,
> But our intercourse will grow
> Through detente, as detente
> Brings complete cooperation.
> By the way, may we say
> We adore your little nation,
> And with heavy cannon
> Wish you an un-
> Ending please hello!!!

SCENE 3

The Admirals exit. Upstage of Lord Abe the Imperial court at Kyoto is revealed—the puppet/Emperor, older now, the Priest, and the Two Nobles. Abe kneels and bows before the Emperor. The Priest manipulates the puppet's arms.

PRIEST: The Americans did not come—

ABE: No, my lord.

PRIEST: And yet they have come back.

FIRST NOBLE: Along with Frenchmen, Englishmen—

SECOND NOBLE: All manner of barbarian invaders—

PRIEST: Soon our country will be overrun.

ABE: My lords, please. You must not upset the Emperor with these petty affairs of state. They are the Shogunate's responsibility.

PRIEST: Yes, they are.

ABE: I assure you, my lords. There is no difficulty with these foreigners. And if there is, I shall attend to it.

RECITER: So says the Shogun. There are those who would say otherwise.

(A drum beat, and the Lords of the South enter down the hanamichi)

The Lords of the South. What can have brought them to the Emperor's court in this time of national crisis?

(The Lords of the South bow before the Emperor)

FIRST LORD: With the Emperor's permission.

SECOND LORD: Brought here to amuse his holiness, the southern provinces' most celebrated storyteller—

FIRST LORD: With the Emperor's permission.

ABE: The Emperor appreciates your thoughtfulness, my lords, but he is tired, and—

PRIEST *(Interrupting)*: The Emperor grants his permission.

(Abe is taken aback. The Lords address the Imperial court directly)

SECOND LORD: May it please his holiness—

FIRST LORD: A brief tale, especially selected for our young Emperor during this barbarian invasion—

(The Reciter moves to the storyteller's spot and tells the tale)

STORYTELLER *(Slowly opening a fan)*: The Tale of the Courageous King. Long ago and far away, behind the highest mountain peak, there lay a magic land of peace and harmony, ruled by a young king, little more than a child. One day, a royal hunting party set out from the young king's palace in search of tigers near the river bank. While his hunters beat the bush, the King retired to a sunny glade, and sipped green tea—

(The fan becomes a cup)

—prepared by his companion, his Lord High Protector. Around his head buzzed sleepy bees—

(The closed fan describes a graceful arc around his head)

—and past him darted brilliant butterflies.

(The fan is opened and becomes a butterfly)

Then suddenly the butterflies were gone—for like the young King they heard the beaters drawing closer through the bush.

(The fan floats up, is quickly closed, then slapped down rhythmically in the Storyteller's hand to sound like beaters)

Deep in the forest, the underbrush began to dip and wave—

(The fan becomes the underbrush)

—and snapping twigs—

(Several snaps from the fan)

—and tearing leaves all heralded the beast's approach! The Lord Protector drew his sword to meet the tiger's rush—

(The fan becomes the sword)

—the bamboo trees were thrust aside and there appeared—no tiger, but a man! Then two men, three, then more than one could count. Bearded ogres with gray skin and matted hair, waving swords and spears. "We are emissaries from the Kingdom of the Giants, come to open up your backward land!" When he heard that, the Lord Protector cast aside his sword and fled. The King was left alone. Oh, what will become of him, abandoned by his treacherous protector? Surely the savages from across the sea will cut him down! But look . . . how superbly he stands his ground! Look how his sword leaps from its scabbard! One invader—gored in the stomach! Another! See how the head flies from the body! Another! And another! Now hear the shouts, hear the roars of defiance as the King's faithful beaters rush to his side. All join in the fray as the screams of the dying savages echo and re-echo down the forest ravine. Oh yes, here was a great victory—for in an hour not a single barbarian was left alive, as once again the butterflies returned to float and shimmer over the wild flowers, dyed crimson by the blood of

foreigners. And then, just as the young King
sheathed his sword, into the glade strode a
magnificent tiger. "Your Majesty," the tiger said, "I
am the king of all the jungle beasts. But from the
forest I have watched you fight these Western
dogs, and surely you, and you alone, deserve to
wear the royal crown." So saying, he kow-towed
and led the hunters in a shout: "All Hail the King!
All Hail our Courageous King!"

*(The Lords of the South quietly applaud, then turn
toward the Emperor and quietly repeat the phrase)*

LORDS OF THE SOUTH: All hail the king, all hail our
courageous king.
PRIEST & NOBLES *(Joining them)*: All hail the king, all hail
our courageous king.

(Abe remains impassive. Blackout)

SCENE 4

*Kayama and Manjiro kneel at either side of the stage
before small, delicate Japanese tables. Both men wear
traditional robes. Kayama is writing on a small scroll
with a brush. Occasionally he dips the brush into a
shallow lacquer ink bowl. Beneath his table is a box.
Arranged in front of Manjiro is the paraphernalia for the
tea ceremony—an earthenware cup, a tea caddy, a
bamboo spoon, a bamboo whisk. Next to him is a cast-iron
kettle and brazier stand, with a bamboo dipper. Manjiro
contemplates these objects silently.*

RECITER: Two men, whose fortunes have been altered by
the Westerners' arrival. Manjiro, the common fisher-

man made samurai. And Kayama Yesaemon, the
minor samurai made governor.

(Reading as Kayama writes)

A letter from Kayama Yesaemon to the Shogun.
My Lord Abe. It is my privilege to inform you of
the current state of our relationship with
foreigners here in Uraga.

*(Kayama removes a bowler hat from the box under his
table and examines it)*

As you have doubtless learned from servants far
more worthy than myself, there are now two
hundred Westerners among us. Five times as many
as a year ago—when they first came.

KAYAMA *(Sings)*:
    It's called a bowler hat.
    I have no wife.
    The swallow flying through the sky
    Is not as swift as I
    Am, flying through my life.
    You pour the milk before the tea.
    The Dutch ambassador is no fool.
    I must remember that.

    *(Stagehands enter and replace Kayama's writing brush
    with a steel pen. They add a line or two to his face.
    Manjiro is similarly aged, but everything else about him
    remains unchanged. The Reciter continues with Kayama's
    letter)*

RECITER: Three years ago we set aside one district of the
    town for Westerners, and yet we are still unable to
    provide them with residences which they consider
    suitable. For this I humbly ask your indulgence.

KAYAMA:

> I wear a bowler hat.
> They send me wine.
> The house is far too grand.
> I've bought a new umbrella stand.
> Today I visited the church beside the shrine.
> I'm learning English from a book.
> Most exciting.
> It's called a bowler hat.

> *(Stagehands add a touch of gray to Kayama's and Manjiro's hair. Manjiro begins the tea ceremony. Meanwhile Kayama's table is replaced by a more Western one. He is given a chair. During all this the Reciter reads)*

RECITER: Of all the Westerners with whom I have to deal, the merchants are most worrisome. They import goods we do not need, and export those we cannot do without. Last month they bought and shipped to Shanghai so much flour that the price here almost tripled. The noodlemakers were affected most severely and threatened to set fire to the Western warehouses. I found it necessary to restrain them.

> *(Kayama takes a watch from his pocket)*

KAYAMA:

> It's called a pocket watch.
> I have a wife.
> No eagle flies against the sky
> As eagerly as I
> Have flown against my life.
> One smokes American cigars.
> The Dutch ambassador was most rude.
> I will remember that.

> *(As Manjiro continues the tea ceremony, Stagehands place*

a nineteenth-century tea service on Kayama's table, and pour him a cup of tea which he sweetens and lightens)

RECITER: Although the Westerners have been in residence for upwards of six years now, our samurai still mistake their foreign manners for disrespect. To avoid unpleasant incidents, I have required all samurai to remove their swords before entering the city.

KAYAMA:
I wind my pocket watch.
We serve white wine.
The house is far too small.
I killed a spider on the wall.
One of the servants thought it was a lucky sign.
I read Spinoza every day.
Formidable.
Where is my bowler hat?

(Stagehands replace Kayama's table with a desk and revolving chair. The hat is removed. Manjiro sips from his cup three times, rests, then finishes it)

RECITER: I will not bother you with details of the rowdy sailors and adventurers who plague our port. As you know, provisions of the treaties which you signed eight years ago make it impossible for me to deal with them. But fortunately, the behavior of the foreign consuls and ambassadors themselves has been above reproach. They have built themselves a club, complete with bar and billiard room. And only gentlemen may enter.

(Kayama slowly spins around in his chair; he sports a monocle)

KAYAMA:
It's called a monocle.

I've left my wife.
No bird exploring in the sky
Explores as well as I
The corners of my life.
One must keep moving with the times.
The Dutch ambassador is a fool.
He wears a bowler hat.

(Manjiro finishes the ceremony, rises and dresses himself for sword practice. A French oil painting is hung on the screen behind Kayama)

RECITER: My lord, here in Uraga we have reached an understanding with the Westerners. Of course I wish them gone, but while they remain I shall try to turn their presence into an advantage rather than a burden. Last week I joined them in a fox hunt.

(Kayama puts on glasses)

KAYAMA:
They call them spectacles.
I drink much wine.
I take imported pills.
I have a house up in the hills
I've hired British architects to redesign.
One must accommodate the times
As one lives them.
One must remember that.

RECITER: Your humble servant, Kayama Yesaemon.

(A Servant runs on with a gray tailcoat, and holds it out to Kayama)

KAYAMA:
It's called a cutaway . . .

(He exits, followed by the Servant; a beat, then Manjiro exits, completely dressed as a samurai)

SCENE 5

Manjiro enters, followed by an Older Samurai. The Two Men are fencing, Manjiro taking a lesson from the Older Man. A beautiful Girl enters behind them, carrying tea things on a small low table.

GIRL: Father.

OLDER SWORDSMAN: Manjiro has not yet finished with his exercises. Leave the table there.

(The Girl puts the table down, bows, and crosses Upstage to an imaginary garden, intermittently dipping to the floor and pulling out from her kimono sleeve an azalea. The effect is almost that of a dance. Downstage, the Swordsmen resume their fencing, silently this time—in mime)

RECITER: The ancient art of kenjutsu, still practiced by the faithful samurai who have not yet had their heads turned by the wonders of the West.

(He follows the fencing for a moment, emitting an occasional shout or grunt for the silent Swordsmen.

Upstage of the Girl, a Stagehand enters and places a small wall, 2' high and 3' long. Gracefully, delicately, the Girl continues plucking flowers from her sleeve while the Swordsmen fence. Upstage of the wall, Three British Sailors enter)

FIRST SAILOR: 'Ello, look at this.

SECOND SAILOR: That's a lovely piece of work.

FIRST SAILOR: D'ya suppose she's one of those geisha girls?

THIRD SAILOR: 'Ere, we'll soon find out. Give us a leg up.

(Wooden blocks are beaten at the side of the stage, and

the Swordsmen disappear Downstage Right, reappearing Upstage Left and crossing Right.

The Sailors disappear Upstage Right, reappear Downstage and enter Left.

A Stagehand places the wall Downstage; another, the tea table Upstage. In other words, Upstage Right becomes Downstage Left.

The wood blocks stop)

FIRST SAILOR : 'Ello, look at this.

SECOND SAILOR: That's a lovely piece of work.

FIRST SAILOR: D'ya suppose she's one of those geisha girls?

THIRD SAILOR: 'Ere, we'll soon find out. Give us a leg up.

(He vaults the fence and then helps the others over. He crosses to the Girl)

Don't be afraid. We don't mean you any 'arm. 'Arry's my name and these two are my mates.

(The Two Sailors tip their hats and smile)

What pretty flowers. D'ya suppose that I could have one?

(She gives him one)

Thank you. That's lovely.

FIRST SAILOR: 'Ere. And one for his mates?

THIRD SAILOR: There's a nice lady.

SECOND SAILOR: Much obliged.

THIRD SAILOR *(Sings)*:
    Pretty lady in the pretty garden, cantcher stay?
    Pretty lady, we got leave and we got paid today.
    Pretty lady with the flower,
    Give a lonely sailor 'alf an hour.

Pretty lady, can you understand a word I say?
Don't go away.

FIRST SAILOR *(Sings)*:
Pretty lady, you're the cleanest thing I seen all year.

THIRD SAILOR *(Sings)*:
I sailed the world for you.

FIRST SAILOR:
Pretty lady, you're enough to make me glad I'm here.

(Simultaneously)

SECOND SAILOR:
Pretty lady, could I hear you laugh,
I ain't heard a lady laugh for I don't know how long.
I'll sing a song for you,
Tell you tales of adventuring, strange and fantastical.
Pretty lady, I ain't never been away from home.
Pretty lady, beg your pardon,
Wontcher walk me through your pretty garden?

THIRD SAILOR:
Pretty lady, I'm a million miles from Stepney Green.
You are the softest thing I ever seen.
Stay with me please, I been away so long.
Don't be afraid . . . hey . . .
No, listen, pretty lady, beg your pardon,
Wontcher walk me through your pretty garden?

FIRST SAILOR:
Pretty lady, how about it?
Dontcher know how long I been without it?
Pretty lady in the garden, wotcher say?
Cantcher stay? . . . Hey, wait, don't go yet.
Pretty lady with the pretty bow,
Please don't go, it's early.
Wontcher walk me through your pretty garden?

ALL SAILORS:
> Pretty lady, look I'm on my knees,
> Pretty please.

FIRST SAILOR *(Speaks)*: What do we do now?
THIRD SAILOR: I think we're supposed to offer money.

> *(Holding all his money out to her)*

> 'Ere, is this enough?

> *(She cowers)*

> No? Come on blokes, cough it up. 'Ow's this? Is this enough?

> *(They are surrounding her)*

> 'Tsall we've got. Please?

SECOND SAILOR *(Sings)*:
> Pretty lady in the pretty garden, wontcher stay?

FIRST AND SECOND SAILOR *(Sing)*:
> Pretty lady, we got leave and we got paid today.

FIRST SAILOR:
> Pretty lady with the flower . . .

ALL:
> Give a lonely sailor 'alf an hour.

FIRST SAILOR:
> Pretty lady in the pretty garden, wontcher stay?

SECOND SAILOR:
> Pretty lady in the pretty garden, wontcher stay?

THIRD SAILOR:
> Pretty lady in the pretty garden, wotcher say?

FIRST SAILOR:
> Why can't you stay?

SECOND SAILOR:
I sailed the world for you . . .

THIRD SAILOR:
Don't go away . . .

GIRL *(Calls in alarm)*: Father!
OLDER SWORDSMAN *(Standing and turning)*: What is this?
THIRD SAILOR: Pardon me, sir. 'Arry's the name. I'm afraid there's been a—

> *(The Older Swordsman cuts the Third Sailor down. The others run, but the First Sailor is slashed by the Swordsman as he scrambles back over the wall.*
>
> *Stagehands enter and clear the stage)*

SCENE 6

RECITER: The murder of these English sailors is no isolated incident. In Yokohama, a French diplomat is set upon by samurai and cut to pieces. In Osaka, two German merchants are dragged from their club and disemboweled. The foreign powers rage and thunder, threatening to invade if the attacks continue. What is to be done? What can Lord Abe do, caught between the Westerners and the rebellious samurai who would expel them? The country trembles on the brink of anarchy!

The Tokaido, the royal road from Edo to Kyoto. As they travel to the Emperor's court, Kayama Yesaemon reports to the Shogun on the murder of the British sailors.

(Kayama, Lord Abe and a Samurai Bodyguard enter, followed by Bearers carrying a pair of palanquins)

ABE: You are sure that the indemnity was properly delivered?

KAYAMA: My lord, I gave it to the English Ambassador myself.

ABE: And he was satisfied?

KAYAMA: With the money, yes my lord. But he insisted that he receive the Emperor's apology to Queen Victoria in three days' time.

ABE: He shall. We will have the Emperor seal the letter of apology tonight, then send it back to Edo by our fastest runners. What about the samurai who cut the sailors down?

KAYAMA: They have been reprimanded, my lord. But it seemed unwise to punish them. Certain lords, the Lords of the South, are treating them as heroes, calling them the true defenders of Japan.

(Abe snorts)

There is a phrase, my lord. A slogan that they have adopted. "Restore the Emperor and Expel the Barbarians."

ABE *(Bitterly)*: Any fool can argue that the Westerners should be expelled. Expelling them is something else again.

(Pause)

What do these Lords propose? That we attack the English cannon with our swords? That we sink the Russian steamships with our pikes? There is only one way. We must appease the Westerners until we have learned the secrets of their power and success. Then, when we have become their equals. Then, perhaps. Then, if we are sure the time is right—

(A Stagehand enters and indicates falling rain with a

fluttering fan. Abe gestures to the Bearers, who pause as he and Kayama climb into the palanquins; to the Bearers)

You there, close up these palanquins before we are soaked through to the skin.

(Suddenly Four Assassins appear)

ABE: What is it?

(The Bearers run as the Assassins attack. As the fight rages, Abe is killed in his palanquin. Finally the Samurai Bodyguard kills the last Assassin. He and Kayama then cross to Abe's body and examine it)

KAYAMA *(Sheathing his sword)*: These were no ordinary bandits. They were assassins.

SAMURAI: Look at the crests beneath their cloaks and you will see who sent them.

KAYAMA: The Lords of the South!

SAMURAI: "Restore the Emperor—"

(A Cloaked Figure, who has remained in the background, now steps forward)

CLOAKED FIGURE *(Completing the Samurai's phrase)*: "Expel the Barbarians."

(The Cloaked Figure and the Samurai fight, and the Samurai is killed. The Cloaked Figure then removes his wraps and reveals himself as Manjiro)

KAYAMA: Manjiro! You—one of them? You, who were the first to welcome the Americans.

MANJIRO: What was I then? An ignorant country boy, less than an animal. What am I now? Will you draw your sword as a fellow samurai or shall I cut you down like the Western dog you have become?

KAYAMA: I should have known! Conspirator—murderer—fisherman!

*(They fight. Kayama is killed. The Two Nobles enter at
the rear of the hanamichi carrying the Emperor—a
larger, older version of the puppet from earlier scenes.
The Nobles put the puppet/Emperor down at Center
Stage, then bow as the Lords of the South follow them
down the hanamichi)*

FIRST LORD: We are greatly pleased, Manjiro. The Emperor will not forget his debt to you.

SECOND LORD: With the Shogun dead, Japan will be Japan again.

*(The Lords kneel on either side of the Emperor and pick
up the sticks which manipulate his arms)*

FIRST LORD: We will kill the Western merchants.

SECOND LORD: We will burn their embassies!

FIRST LORD: In the name of the Emperor we will drive them back into the sea!

LORDS: In the name of the Emperor—

*(The Lords are suddenly interrupted by a voice from the
puppet/Emperor)*

EMPEROR'S VOICE: In the name of the Emperor—enough!

*(Long pause as they stare at the puppet. Magically, real
hands emerge from the sleeves, break off the puppet sticks,
and toss them away. Then the hands strip away the mask,
revealing the face of the Reciter. As he continues
speaking, Stagehands enter and remove layer upon layer
of his imperial robes)*

RECITER/EMPEROR: The day when others speak for me is past. From now on, my word shall be law. And mine alone. I am the Emperor Meiji. Rise—and listen! No more will we draw sword, one Japanese against another. Those who have committed murder in my name have been misguided. In the future they will be restrained—along with those who have encouraged them. Rise!

(The Nobles, the Lords of the South—everyone on stage begins to rise slowly and listen)

From this day forth, all samurai will put aside their swords and cease to wear their crested robes.

(Stagehands remove Manjiro's swords and robes. They sever his samurai's topknot with a knife)

They will take up useful trades. Rise!

(The Reciter/Emperor's final layer of robes is removed. Beneath it he wears the gold braid and buttons of a nineteenth-century Western general. He turns to the audience. Pause)

Yes.

(Pause)

In the name of progress we will turn our backs on ancient ways. We will cast aside our feudal forms, eliminate all obstacles which hinder our development.

(Music begins as the stage is cleared, leaving the Reciter/ Emperor alone with a Chorus of Three)

We will organize an army and a navy, equipped with the most modern weapons. And when the time is right, we will send forth expeditions to visit with our less enlightened neighbors. We will open up Formosa, Korea, Manchuria and China. We will do for the rest of Asia what America has done for us!

CHORUS *(Sings)*:
Streams are flowing.

See what's coming
Next!

RECITER/EMPEROR: We will build railroads, foundries, telegraphs and steamships.

(More Chorus enter)

CHORUS:
Winds are blowing.
See what's coming,
See what's going
Next!

RECITER/EMPEROR: Factories will spring up all across our land.

(More Chorus enter)

CHORUS:
Roads are turning,
Journey with them.
A little learning—
Next!

RECITER/EMPEROR: Foreign architects will reconstruct our cities.

(The Chorus is enlarged by Three Contemporary Japanese Businessmen)

BUSINESSMEN:
Waters churning,
Lightning flashes.
Kings are burning,
Sift the ashes . . .
Next!

RECITER/EMPEROR: The day will come when the Western powers will be forced to acknowledge us as their undisputed equals.

(The entire stage begins to fill with Contemporary Japanese Figures, everything from Women in pantsuits to Teenagers in leather jackets)

COMPANY:
> Tower tumbles,
> Tower rises—
> Next!

RECITER/EMPEROR: And all of this will be achieved— sooner than you think!

COMPANY:
> Tower crumbles,
> Man revises.
> Motor rumbles,
> Civilizes.
> More surprises
> Next!
>
> Learn the lesson
> From the master.
> Add the sugar,
> Spread the plaster.
> Do it nicer,
> Do it faster . . .
> Next!

RECITER *(Who has stripped off his Emperor's uniform, and stands in plain black pants and t-shirt)*:
> The practical bird,
> Having no tree of its own,
> Borrows another's.

COMPANY:
> Streams are roaring,
> Overspilling—
> Next!

Old is boring,
New is thrilling,
Keep exploring—
Next!

First the thunder—
Just a murmur—
A little blunder—
Next!
Then the wonder—
See how pretty!
(Going under—
What a pity!)
Next!

Streams are flying,
Use the motion—
Next!
Streams are drying—
Mix a potion.
Streams are dying—
Try the ocean.
Brilliant notion—
Next!

Never mind a small disaster.
Who's the stronger, who's the faster?
Let the pupil show the master—
Next!
Next!

A VOICE: There are 223 Japan Air Lines ticket offices in 153 cities throughout the world.

COMPANY:
Next!

ANOTHER VOICE: There are eight Toyota dealerships in

the city of Detroit, and Seiko watch is the third best selling watch in Switzerland.

COMPANY:
Next!

THIRD VOICE: Of the 196 new restaurants that opened in New York City last year, 61 were sushi bars!

COMPANY:
Next!

FOURTH VOICE: The Tokaido Express, the world's fastest train, can now carry passengers along the royal route from Tokyo to Kyoto in two hours and three minutes!

COMPANY:
Next!

FIFTH VOICE: Next spring, Mitsubishi will market video cassettes of cherry trees, so that people may view the cherry blossoms in the comfort of their own homes!

COMPANY:
Next!

SIXTH VOICE: In 1985, half a million Americans, four hundred thousand Europeans and one million other Asians will visit Japan!

COMPANY:
Next!

Never mind a small disaster!
Who's the stronger, who's the faster?
Let the pupil show the master
Next!
Next!
Next!
Next!

Next!
Next!

(There is a frenzied dance, suddenly interrupted by the Reciter)

RECITER: Nippon. The Floating Kingdom.

(Wood blocks usher on the traditionally dressed figures of Kayama and Tamate, who pass silently through the Company)

There was a time when foreigners were not welcome here. But that was long ago. One hundred and thirty years.

(Pause)

Welcome to Japan.

COMPANY *(Singing)*:
    Next! Next!
    Brilliant notions,
    Still improving—
    Next! Next!
    Make the motions,
    Keep it moving—
    Next!
    Next!
    Next!
    Next!

                    BLACKOUT